MEDIEVAL LITERATURE

THE BASICS

Medieval Literature: The Basics is an engaging introduction to this fascinating body of literature. The volume breaks down the variety of genres used in the corpus of medieval literature and makes these texts accessible to readers. It engages with the familiarities present in the narratives and connects these ideas with a contemporary, twenty-first century audience. The volume also addresses contemporary medievalism to show the presence of medieval literature in contemporary culture, such as film, television, games, and novels.

From Dante and Chaucer to Christine de Pisan, this book deals with questions such as:

- What is medieval literature?
- What are some of the key topics and genres of medieval literature?
- How did it evolve as technology, such as the printing press, developed?
- How has it remained relevant in the twenty-first century?

Medieval Literature: The Basics is an ideal introduction for students coming to the subject for the first time, while also acting as a springboard from which deeper interaction with medieval literature can be developed.

Angela Jane Weisl is Professor of English and Director of Graduate Studies at Seton Hall University, USA. She is the author of *Conquering the Reign of Femeny: Gender and Genre in Chaucer's Romance* (1995), *The Persistence of Medievalism: Narrative Adventures in Contemporary Culture* (2003), and with Tison Pugh, *Medievalisms: Making the Past in the Present* (2012), as well as many articles on a wide variety of medieval subjects.

Anthony Joseph Cunder graduated from Seton Hall University, USA with a Master's in English. He has published work (both fiction and scholarly articles) in a variety of online and print journals in addition to publishing a memoir about growing up and living with type 1 diabetes.

The Basics

For a full list of titles in this series, please visit www.routledge.com/The-Basics/book-series/B

MEDIEVAL LITERATURE

THE BASICS

Angela Jane Weisl and Anthony Joseph Cunder

Routledge
Taylor & Francis Group

LONDON AND NEW YORK

First published 2018
by Routledge
2 Park Square, Milton Park, Abingdon, Oxon OX14 4RN

and by Routledge
711 Third Avenue, New York, NY 10017

Routledge is an imprint of the Taylor & Francis Group, an informa business

© 2018 Angela Jane Weisl and Anthony Joseph Cunder

British Library Cataloguing in Publication Data
A catalogue record for this book is available from the British Library

Library of Congress Cataloging in Publication Data
Names: Weisl, Angela Jane, 1963- author. | Cunder, A. J. (Anthony Joseph), author.
Title: Medieval literature : the basics / Angela Jane Weisl, Anthony Joseph Cunder.
Other titles: Basics (Routledge (Firm))
Description: Abingdon, Oxon ; New York, NY : Routledge, 2018. | Series: The basics | Includes bibliographical references and index.
Identifiers: LCCN 2017047343 | ISBN 9781138669048 (hardback : alk. paper) | ISBN 9781138669055 (pbk. : alk. paper) | ISBN 9781317210634 (epub) | ISBN 9781317210627 (mobipocket)
Subjects: LCSH: Literature, Medieval--History and criticism.
Classification: LCC PN671 .W45 2018 | DDC 809/.02--dc23
LC record available at https://lccn.loc.gov/2017047343

ISBN: 978-1-138-66904-8 (hbk)
ISBN: 978-1-138-66905-5 (pbk)
ISBN: 978-1-315-61833-3 (ebk)

Typeset in Bembo
by Taylor & Francis Books

CONTENTS

ACKNOWLEDGEMENTS

Medieval Literature: The Basics first arose from our mutual love of the Middle Ages. We hope in this volume to instil (or at least inspire) in readers a similar appreciation for a time period that encompasses literature as eclectic and diverse as the peoples that populated its lands. We have also been helped by people as eclectic and diverse as well, and we wish to acknowledge their support with our gratitude. First and foremost, we would like to thank Ruth Hilsdon, Polly Dodson, Zoë Meyer, Emma Craig, Katie Finnegan, and everyone at Routledge: The Basics for their interest in having us for this project and for being so supportive throughout the process, especially with our loose interpretation of "August." The scholars who read the proposal offered helpful suggestions that have made the volume much stronger. Seton Hall University provided tremendous support for the project, particularly with a well-timed Sabbatical in Spring 2017 which allowed us to complete the volume in a timely fashion. Special thanks to (former) Dean Chrysanthy Grieco and (former) Provost Larry Robinson, and doubly special thanks to the English Department for making this Sabbatical possible and for believing in the project's value. Colleagues Mary Balkun, Jonathan Farina, Karen Gevirtz, and Donovan Sherman have been particularly encouraging and helpful. The librarians at Seton Hall have been very helpful in making material easily available and extending access to materials past graduation. Nicole Olivotti provided enormous help with the detail work of the Index.

The community of medieval scholars has been vital in challenging traditional views of the period and its literature; they have been very influential on our perspective and our commitment to putting forward a multicultural, multilingual, multi-racial, and multi-religious vision of the Middle Ages. We would specifically like to acknowledge *The Public Medievalist* and *In the Medieval Middle*, two exceptional blogs that will enrich anyone's study and understanding of this time period. If we can help undermine stereotypes of a rigid, univalent Middle Ages, and show how much richer a diverse and multi-vocal medieval literature is, then this book will be a success. Their information can be found in the "Web Resources" section; they, and the scholars who contribute to them, are vital resources for learning about the field.

On a lighter note, we would also like to thank the Science, Industry, and Business Library (a division of the New York Public Library) for providing the collaborative space in which we met on so many Mondays to research and compile the various chapters of this book (despite the various incidents and excitements that always seemed to occur during our meetings, from unauthorized patrons rearranging library furniture to the prolific snoring emanating from those who sought to take advantage of the library's quiet ambience – before security vigorously shook them awake). We'd also like to extend our appreciation to Andrews Coffee Shop for providing a place to refresh our minds (and stomachs) after our trips to the library – many of our best decisions about the book were made there over grilled cheese sandwiches and green tea.

Finally, to our partners, Bob Squillace and Kyle Augustyniak, who have endlessly listened to us witter on about the Middle Ages, we owe great thanks. But the greatest thanks must be given to each other for making this collaboration such a joy, and to our readers, for giving us a reason to undertake it, our deepest gratitude.

INTRODUCTION
HERE BEGYNNETH GAME: THE BASICS
OF MEDIEVAL LITERATURE

What, exactly, is medieval literature? While that might seem like an obvious question, it bears interrogation. Loosely defined, the Middle Ages began with the Fall of Rome to the Visigoths in the fifth century and ended sometime after the introduction of printing, around 1500 CE. In Europe and beyond, these one thousand years of history were characterized, at least in part, by the spread and adoption of Christianity. However, to say that Europe was entirely Christian during the period is an overstatement, in that it excludes the continuing influence of paganism early in the period as well as the vital influence of Islamic and Jewish communities, both within the borders of Europe and outside, not to mention variations within Christianity itself. Anxieties about these communities and their control of territory that included Christian pilgrimage sites led to the Crusades, starting in 1095, an attempt by Christians to reclaim control of the Holy Land from the Muslims they called Saracens that led to a series of territorial losses and a great deal of devastation, including the sacking of Constantinople in the Fourth Crusade (1202–4) and the elimination of the Albigensians in Provençe (1202–29).

The Middle Ages were certainly a time of significant upheaval, in which systems of government changed (often from tribal to feudal systems, although to suggest that feudalism was the only form of socio-political arrangement is another gross overstatement, and a broader geographic notion of the Middle Ages beyond the borders of Western Europe offers a wider range of political models), conflicts rearranged borders and land-holdings, and violence was often a fact of life. However, there were also significant periods of peace which led to a rise in leisure time and therefore to important bodies of literature, as well as structures of patronage of the arts outside the confines of religious institutions. Cities saw a rise in population in part due to technological and agricultural advances, at least until the devastations of the Bubonic Plague (1346–53), which killed somewhere between 75,000 and 200,000 people in Europe and Asia. Climatologically, the "Medieval Warming Period" led to increased crop yield and allowed the settlement of Greenland by the Norse, although by 1300 the climate was starting to cool, leading to the Little Ice Age that continued into the nineteenth century. Plague, famine, and the Hundred-Years War (1334–1453) among other conflicts characterized the later part of the period.

The Middle Ages also saw a number of significant technological advances, particularly between the twelfth and fourteenth centuries; agriculture, mining, and manufacturing were expanded by developments in water- and wind-mill technology, and building techniques developed significantly from the Romanesque to the Gothic period, characterized by the pointed arches, vaulted roofs, and flying buttresses seen in the European Cathedrals. Crop rotation led to expansion of agriculture, while the use of gunpowder profoundly changed warfare. Mechanical clocks lead to greater precision in the telling of time, and technologies such as eyeglasses and the printing press had significant impact on the literary as well as the social, political, and economic spheres. These developments grew out of a nexus of cross-cultural exchange; interactions between Europe, the Middle East, India, and China led to developments and refinements of these various technological advancements, although some technologies trace their roots to Roman and Byzantine inventions. In the maritime world, ships were also becoming more adapted to extended trips, while inventions like the astrolabe, about which Chaucer writes a treatise, made navigation over longer distances easier. These developments, and the increased use of gunpowder, itself a Chinese invention, are often credited with enabling the exploration and colonization which characterize the Early Modern period.

The term "Middle Ages," or *medium aevum*, was first used by Petrarch (1392–74), himself firmly planted in what we would call the medieval period. About a hundred years later, the term was picked up by politicians and historians Flavio Biondi (1392–1463) and Leonardo Bruno (c. 1370–1444), who used the term to distinguish the past from the period they believed themselves to be a part of, a time of a revival of classical learning and humanism. Of course, the Latin classics never went away during the European Middle Ages, where Ovid, Virgil, Lucan, Statius, and others provided sources and inspiration for theological, moral, romantic, and fantastical works. In the twelfth century, through contact between the Christian and Islamic worlds, the works of Aristotle and Greek scientists became increasingly available and widely studied. Because Southern Spain and Sicily were under Islamic control and had large Jewish and Christian populations, and because of increased contact with Byzantium and the Middle East because of the Crusades, and the travels of explorers/traders like Marco Polo, the interchange of ideas became increasingly common. With the rise of medieval universities, a structure was in place to house, translate, and study these texts. Styles in the plastic arts and architecture, such as the Romanesque, Gothic, Islamic, Mozarabic, Byzantine, and Coptic, were all characteristic of the period and influenced each other, so that the Doge's Palace in Venice (built between 810 and 1442) shows strong influences of the Romanesque, Gothic, and Arabic styles combined.

Medieval literature, the subject of this volume, showed equal variation, as one might expect in a span of a thousand-plus years and multiple languages, countries, and interests. The period produced many thousands of manuscripts, not to mention other kinds of inscribed objects, religious and secular (and sometimes combining the two), some in forms that reached back to older examples and others that were profoundly inventive and new. Works exist in poetry and prose, in long and short forms, in unique manuscripts and in multiple copies, in many languages and varied alphabets. Some stories traveled widely and found expression in many different genres and versions, while others appear to have neither sources nor analogues.

While the literate population was very small, giving great prestige and power to those who could read and write, exposure to stories, through oral traditions and public performance, spread lyrics and narratives widely. Religious institutions were greatly responsible for the production of manuscripts, particularly monasteries in

Europe, but there was a significant body of secular material produced throughout the period. Sometimes contemporary readers find the balance of the sacred and the secular challenging when reading medieval works, but religion emerges as one of the profound ways in which medieval writers sought to understand and explain the world around them.

Another challenge in reading medieval literature is a result of the ravages of time; many of the surviving texts exist in incomplete manuscripts, fragments, and copies. Other challenges come from determining correct texts; the inevitable mistakes produced by scribal error and the difficulty of knowing any individual work's full history adds to its complexity. Many works are by unnamed authors; other authors are named, but their history is lost to time. Even some writers who have become quite famous, such as Marie de France and Gottfried von Strassburg, have left very little trace of their biographies. For contemporary readers accustomed to knowing the details and biographies of the authors they read, reading medieval literature can sometimes be a frustrating experience.

Medieval literature asks a wide range of questions and explores an even wider range of themes; while some of these questions and themes seem deeply time-bound, tied to religious practices or social conventions that no longer carry much currency, many are very much like what literature asks today. Explorations of love, honor, prowess, duty, fame, reputation, faith, salvation, meaning, identity, and place in the world abound in medieval material, even if the methods of undertaking these explorations sometimes seem very distant. However, many of the pleasures of medieval literature come from this very alterity: the strange worlds of the monstrous and the miraculous, the complex structures of tribal society, the devotion to chivalric and other codes of behavior, the literal quests taken for transcendent meaning, and the episodic and often disconnected nature of varying kinds of narrative. On the other hand, there is much that remains familiar about medieval narrative: desire for community and love, eroticism (sometimes as hot and steamy as any scene from *Fifty Shades of Grey*), interest in travel and seeing new places, and engagement with the spiritual world, to name a few.

It is perhaps useful to contrast the Middle Ages and its literature to medieval cathedrals and churches. The buildings, bleached white by time as we see them today, suggest a stark, monochromatic palate that belies their polychromed history (to get a sense of what the cathedrals might have looked like, check out images of the show at Amiens Cathedral which seeks to replicate the polychrome that restorers discovered when cleaning some of the face). The European Middle Ages were not a bastion of whiteness, but instead a multiracial, multilingual, multi-religious period with many different peoples occupying the same space, interacting with each other. Goods and stories traveled great distances; a medieval peasant in a small village church might be praying in front of a painting whose pigments came from as far away as Afghanistan and India. Spices, metals, textiles, foods, jewels, and glass all traveled along trade routes that reached from Ireland to China, and if one person didn't carry them from one end to the other, the exchanges along the way led to chains of contact between very diverse peoples. These encounters, whether as part of trade or part of crusade, were not without conflict; quite a bit of the literature of contact focuses on difference and fear of the other, regardless of the side. However, travel narratives often offer examples of productive exchange, showing that valuable communion happened between peoples from very different worlds. Since so many travelogues focus on telling stories about the different places the traveler encounters, it is evident that travelers carried texts with them as well as goods.

One overt example of textual travel is the story of Siddhartha Gautama, the Buddha, which originates in India and is slowly transformed into the story of Barlaam and Josephat, appearing in Arabic, Greek, Uyghur, Turfanese, Hebrew, German, and French versions (among others), each taking on its own local color, so that by the time Gui de Cambrai writes his version (c. 1220–25) it has become a Christian narrative. Other examples of textual transmission include the stories of *Tristan and Isolde* and of *Floris and Blanchefleur*, which appear in multiple versions and languages across Europe, from Scandinavia to Spain. Legends and romances of Alexander the Great appear in Islamic, Christian, and Jewish versions, with variants in Greek, Persian, Ethiopic, Bulgar, English, French, and Slavonic. The story of *Layla and Majnun*, best known in Nizami's Persian text (c. 1188), circulates from the Caucuses to the interior of Africa, appearing in versions from the Atlantic to the Indian Ocean, and in romances, epics, songs, and poetry. Stories, one imagines, moved in much the same ways as goods, traveling along trade routes and picking up local flavor along the way. So while this volume focuses primarily on Western European literature, it is important to be aware that those texts are connected to a complex network that reaches across a great deal of time and space.

There are many ways to organize an introductory volume to medieval literature, including by chronology and by nation, but because of our interest in the interconnectivity that informs the period, we have chosen instead to focus on genre, loosely defined, and have grouped our chapters around some of the particular themes that structure these genres. Because our job is to introduce the basics of medieval literature, we have focused primarily on the literature of Western Europe, itself primarily Christian, which is what most students are likely to encounter in their courses and what general readers will have heard about. However, this material exists within a much larger textual network to which it is profoundly tied, and we have tried to provide a sense of the other literatures and traditions that form it. To break down the sense of alterity and distance that might make medieval literature seem challenging and remote, or even devoid of interest, we have begun with medievalism – contemporary responses and versions of medieval texts that are likely to be well known. Chapter 1: "Game of Texts: The Magic of Medievalism" teases out the "medieval-ness" of these contemporary creations. We hope to close some of the gap of space and time, bringing historically medieval material a bit closer. After all, most readers approaching medieval literature in this day and age are exposed to it through the many films, video games, and novels that take their inspiration and setting from the time period and retell its core stories for a modern audience. In Chapter 2: "How to Wield a Sword in the Middle Ages: The Literature of War and Violence," we then move to the historical Middle Ages to explore the literature of war and conflict – the epic, the *chanson de geste*, the Icelandic saga, and the literature of chivalry and crusade. Perhaps the largest body of secular literature in the Middle Ages is the courtly romance; this, along with its lyric antecedents and the fabliau which parodies it, is discussed in Chapter 3: "Chivalry is Not Dead: The Literature of Love and Desire." Chapter 4: "Touching Heaven: The Literature of Religion" considers the more literary (as opposed to theological) spiritual genres such as religious lyric, spiritual autobiography, hagiographies, and visionary literature, while Chapter 5: "Meeting Monsters on the Map: The Literature of Space and Time" considers travelogues, historiographies, pilgrimage literature, and chronicles. Finally, we consider some of the major authors of the period in Chapter 6: "The Most Extreme: Iconic Authors of the Middle Ages," which includes figures like Dante and Chaucer, whose body of work prevents them from being confined to any single, genre-defined chapter. In the ludic spirit of many of these famous works, we offer the final chapter as a game; what elements constitute a "major" or iconic author in the Middle Ages? We hope that in this same spirit, readers will come to play their own games with medieval literature, and find in it the same pleasures that have drawn us to this subject. Each chapter ends with suggestions for further reading, and offers a mix of primary and secondary sources, some classic and some more contemporary.

Some of the pleasures of these texts include a way to look back in time and experience the magic of another age without ever having to leave the comfort of our homes. The Middle Ages – perhaps because so many contemporary fantasies use the medieval period as a background for witchcraft, wizardry, and dragons – seem a fitting playground to explore the fantastical. Even many texts produced in the era incorporate the magic of headless horsemen, greedy dragons, and powerful warlocks as nonchalantly as a history textbook today might speak of Guy Fawkes planning the Gunpowder Plot or George Washington crossing the Delaware. Whether or not the people of the Middle Ages actually believed in the existence of magical creatures isn't the point – the magic of reading these texts is itself a journey, a trip back in time to a world that superficially seems so fundamentally different from our own and yet created the foundation upon which the Renaissance and ultimately the twenty-first century were built. The people and characters we read in Chaucer may seem distant in the way they speak and perhaps even the way they think, and yet their humanity – the same humanity that struggles and thrives and breathes today – truly vibrates just beneath the surface of the page.

The literature of the Middle Ages can transport readers to fascinating places and times, rife with ribald humor, illicit rendezvous, passionate romance, undaunted gallantry, and peeks into a world without running water or modern construction. Incredible castles rose without the aid of machines, their towers touching the sky, all from the work of human hands. Stories flourished (though few people were literate enough to read them), transmitted and transcribed across borders. Identities shifted and changed, all without the benefit of modern psychology. The Middle Ages, though distant in time and space, can offer truths and tales that still resonate today. And while we might originally be drawn to the more fantastical Middle Ages (how many medievalists cite *Lord of the Rings* and the like as their entry-point into the historical material?), the literature also feeds many other interests – in religion, in gender and power, in sexuality and desire, in the construction of race, in the uses and understandings of non-human voices, in the rhetoric of disability, in the study of landscape and the environment, in the history of conflict and resolution, and in the development of conflicts that continue today.

Medieval literature provides distinct pleasures for the casual reader, but perhaps even more for the student and scholar, who will find that these texts can be effectively analyzed with any critical theory or approach that they find engaging; doing so not only opens up the complexity of the literature but also enriches the theory as well. The rewards of reading this material are great, and the rewards of studying it perhaps even greater. Ultimately, our hope is that this volume will demystify a body of literature that is too often viewed as foreign and innately different. We want to energize readers of medieval texts and, hopefully, spark a desire to investigate the intricacies, nuances, insights, and influences of these medieval authors to a greater extent by highlighting the value and academic significance they offer students of the Middle Ages. So, journey with us through time and space as we explore the basics of medieval literature and learn how the knights and princesses, the kings and queens, the peasants and farmers, who, in their quests for self-worth, identity, love, and God are perhaps not so different from ourselves.

FOR FURTHER READING

If you feel that you would like to explore medieval literature by reading a range of works (all Western), you might start with the **Anthology of Medieval Literature. (2013). Ed. Rebecca Berg**

Manor. London: Beautiful Feet Books. For more information about reading medieval literature, particularly for the student, consider, **Andrew Galloway. (2007).** *Medieval Literature: A Student Guide.* **London: Bloomsbury**. Another useful resource is **Theodore L. Steinberg's (2003).** *Reading the Middle Ages.* **Jefferson, NC: McFarland**. For further background on the literary Middle Ages, **Pamela King's (2011).** *Medieval Literature 1300–1500.* **Edinburgh: Edinburgh University Press** is helpful, although this work addresses only the High- or Late-Middle Ages, as does **Janet Coleman's (1981).** *Medieval Readers and Writers: Literature and Society 1350–1400.* **New York: Columbia University Press**. Coleman addresses who read and wrote in the Middle Ages – a sense of the reading populace and the authors who provided literary entertainment gives a valuable sense of the material in its time. To consider the point of reading medieval literature in the modern world, and how the past might speak to the present through it, we recommend *Why the Middle Ages Matter: Medieval Light on Modern Injustice.* **(2012) Ed. Celia Chazelle, Simon Doubleday, Felice Lifshitz, and Amy G. Remensnyder. London: Routledge**. This can provide some answers about the point of undertaking a study of medieval literature in a broader context.

GAME OF TEXTS
THE MAGIC OF MEDIEVALISM

If you have purchased a book called *Medieval Literature: The Basics*, there is a good chance that you feel like you don't know much about medieval literature, although it also suggests you are eager to learn more. You might know some names (Chaucer, Dante, Marie de France) and some themes (King Arthur, Knights in Shining Armor, Religion) but you likely are reading this because you feel like you need more background. There is certainly a great deal about medieval literature that you will learn from reading this volume, but you likely already know more than you think. The Middle Ages are having a vogue in contemporary culture: from *The Lord of the Rings* films to *Game of Thrones*, the period, or a fantasy of the period, has lately been occupying a great deal of screen time. Medieval movies, novels, video games, and television programs abound. The period appears in many other genres as well, including operas, fine arts, and architecture, among other forms. This post-medieval body of work that references the Middle Ages, called "medievalism," is many people's introduction to the Middle Ages. We wanted to begin with some contemporary responses to the medieval as a touchstone to establish a few key ideas, vocabulary, and concepts. So join us in this chapter – and in this book – as we travel back in time.

Tom Shippey has famously identified medievalism as:

> the study of responses to the Middle Ages at all periods since a sense of the mediaeval began to develop. Such responses include, but are not restricted to, the activities of scholars, historians and philologists in rediscovering medieval materials;... and artistic creations, whether

literary, visual or musical, based on whatever has been or is thought
to have been recovered from the medieval centuries. The Middle Ages
remain present, moreover, in the modern consciousness, both
through scholarship and through popular media such as film, video
games, poster art, TV series and comic strips, and these media are
also a legitimate object of study, if often intertwined with more tradi-
tionally scholarly topics.

(*Studies in Medievalism* website: 2017, www.medievalism.net/
conferences)

As part of the study of medieval literature, it is important to consider how what is often perceived as distant, archaic, and irrelevant
is still vibrant and present in our own world today.

Based on students' reactions to the Medieval Literature course at
our university, it seems clear that it is a subject they think they do
not know much about. Some students have encountered a little
Chaucer in a British Survey course or some Dante in their Core
Curriculum, but even they feel like they are embarking into
uncharted territory. In fact, they often admit, they have no idea
what they are getting into and are only there because the class meets
at a convenient time or satisfies a requirement. However, a quick
survey reveals that students actually know more about medieval
literature than they think; even if they have not read *The Lord of
the Rings* or *Harry Potter* or *Game of Thrones,* they have seen the
movies or TV shows. Maybe they have enjoyed Brian Helgeland's
A Knight's Tale (2001) or Ridley Scott's *Kingdom of Heaven* (2005)
or have played the early iterations of *Assassin's Creed* or *Dragon Age.*
Or perhaps they have watched sports or gone to a Renaissance Fair
or visited a Hall of Fame somewhere. Or their parents have made
them watch *Monty Python and the Holy Grail* (1975). All of these, as
contemporary as they may seem, and as un-literary as some may
appear on the surface, in some form (intentionally or not) draw
their inspiration from medieval literature. So, if the texts we will
be talking about in the rest of this volume seem like artifacts of a
distant past, in fact they still remain very much alive today.

Medievalism exists in many forms, all of it a kind of fantasy of a
past narrowed down to certain traits. These can be frightening:
many supremacist organizations, such as the Ku Klux Klan, trace
their origins to a fictionally unitary, white Middle Ages that never

existed, and crusade rhetoric has been revived on both sides as conflicts between the West and groups like ISIS and Al-Qaeda have escalated. Other forms also reduce the Middle Ages' complexity, rendering a pagan fantasy seen at Renaissance Fairs (which collapse the Middle Ages and what follows into a blurred past of wenches and turkey legs and costumes) or a past of closed-mindedness and violence. Alternatively, medievalism can be found in the ways in which medieval artifacts are displayed or performed; medieval history can be repurposed to tell a variety of different stories. Medieval combat is reappearing in the Battle of the Nations and the revival of full-contact jousting; yet of course the Battle isn't a real war because nobody dies, and the jousting tournaments are ends in themselves rather than knightly training for real combat to come. None of these fantasies are truly accurate to the Middle Ages; the kernels of truth within them, while interesting, are often very isolated from their contexts and exaggerated to mean something else. And yet, one thing they tell us is that there are multiple kinds of long- ings which the imagined Middle Ages fulfill. Because this volume is particularly concerned with the Middle Ages' imagination of its own time in the form of its literature, our attention will focus here on genres which draw specifically from medieval literature, or which themselves use narrative to tell medieval stories. Works of medievalism of varying kinds abound for those who wish to pursue this study further.

EPIC FANTASY AND THE MIDDLE AGES

In J.R.R. Tolkien's essay on what has come to be known today as "fantasy" literature, he states that there is a "desire to escape, not indeed from life, but from our present time and self-made misery" (Tolkien 1983: 151). He goes on to explain how fantasy – or "fairy stories," as he calls them – is an escapist genre, giving readers the opportunity to "fly from the noise, stench, ruthlessness, and extra- vagance of the internal-combustion engine" for a time and to "visit, free as a fish, the deep sea" (Tolkien 1983: 151). At its core, the fantasy genre grounds itself in its ability to transport readers to another world, one with different rules or creatures from our own. We can, as Tolkien says, visit the marvels of a medieval castle without ever leaving the comfort of home – we can watch as knights battle from the backs of dragons or perhaps experience one of the "profounder wishes: such as the desire to converse with other living things" (Tolkien 1983: 152) such as animals and beasts.

Although various subgenres of "fantasy" have emerged such as magical realism, urban fantasy, and steampunk – all of which generally take place in a contemporary setting – classic or "epic" fantasy most often requires a medieval background to properly take the name. Tolkien's own pivotal work *The Lord of the Rings* (1954–5) takes place in a medieval world where horses (or eagles) are the only means of conveyance and the hum of the combustion engine is nowhere to be found. Christopher Paolini's *Eragon* and the books that follow (2002–11), another popular fantasy about a boy who finds a dragon egg and becomes a dragon rider, take place in a similar medieval era where the modern innovations of the author's world never appear. Even George R.R. Martin's *Song of Ice and Fire* series (1996–present) (popularized by the HBO televised series *Game of Thrones*) takes place in a medieval world where enchantment and swordplay go hand in hand.

The list of examples goes on and raises the question of why contemporary authors find the Middle Ages such a fitting background against which to tell their magical stories. Is it because Tolkien set the example with his fundamental work that has come to define how we view the fantasy genre? Or is it something deeper, something that Tolkien himself hints at when he describes fairy stories as escapist in nature? Perhaps it can be a combination of the two.

While setting an "escapist" story in a contemporary world can still distract the reader from the unpaid bills piling up on the counter, or the minivan in the driveway that needs an oil change, there is a certain refuge in reading a story that takes place in a truly different world, not only in place but in time as well. There is a subtle magic in reading about elven spellcasters who live among the trees and travel by horseback – a magic even in reading about knights who must defend their castles against an ogre horde. Escaping into a romanticized version of the past – our world's past, we must not forget – offers a charm of its own, and allows authors like Martin, Tolkien, and Paolini to immediately invoke the sentiment and aura of the Middle Ages without spending precious chapters building an entirely new world that science fiction authors, in some ways, must do. While we already know about the past, the future is necessarily a mystery. And while the geography in these fantasy stories will often be different from Medieval Europe, the tropes of feudalism, swordplay, knighthood, castles – even if understood only loosely by contemporary audiences – can be summoned with a sentence.

Additionally, fantasy stories often mimic their medieval counterparts in more than just setting. The themes and models of the medieval romance or epic find resonance in these novels and have become such a staple that no fantasy can be complete without employing some combination of them. These tropes include the quest, the hero, the coming of age both in terms of combat and sexuality, the sense of journey and learning something along the way, and betrayal. All of these abound in medieval texts and can certainly be found in any fantasy story published today, offering a link between the past and the present that goes deeper than the backdrop of castles and the absence of modern plumbing.

And yet, differences also remain between medieval texts and texts that look back to the Middle Ages. The modes of storytelling, for instance, have changed radically from the poets of the premodern eras. While Chaucer, Dante, and their compatriots wrote lengthy works in many genres, their narratives were predominantly linear, focusing on how characters (often limiting the primary protagonist to a single character) moved forward temporally to advance the action. Fantasy epics of today (like Martin's) often have great temporal latitude, following multiple storylines, jumping forward and backward in time, and stretching out narratives for the span of three, four, five, or even twelve books.

Contemporary novels set in a medieval world differ from their historical predecessors in world building as well. It takes great effort to convince a modern reader to suspend his or her disbelief: as Tolkien writes, "To make a Secondary World in which [a] green sun will be credible, will probably require labour and thought, and will certainly demand a special skill, a kind of elvish craft" (Tolkien 1983: 140). Medieval authors, on the other hand, did not have to establish the world in which their stories took place since it was their own, allowing them to focus more on character, plot, and action. This does not mean that medieval texts are devoid of description, but they (obviously) do not need to explain the

Middle Ages. Scenes may be set, and historical contexts established, but the kind of description we think of as commonplace in medieval texts exists only to detail something out of the ordinary, such as the Green Chapel in *Sir Gawain and the Green Knight*. When magic appears in a medieval text, it is given little explanation and the readers must simply take it for granted that enchantment operated as a part of the world that the medieval author created.

Furthermore, as Alex Ross writes in "The Ring and the Rings: Wagner vs. Tolkien," epic fantasy stories set in the Middle Ages have a way of interposing modern concerns upon tales of the past. For instance, Ross writes that:

> it is surely no accident that the notion of a Ring of Power surfaced in the late nineteenth century, when technologies of mass destruction were appearing on the horizon. Pre-modern storytellers had no frame of reference for such things... those with power were born with power, and those without, without.
>
> (Ross 2003)

In crafting a new mythology for England, Tolkien overlays the anxieties of his age with the visceral settings of his country's Germanic past, using "myth [as] a window on an ideal world, both brighter and blacker than our own" (Ross 2003).

MEDIEVAL MOVIES

Tolkien is currently as famous for Peter Jackson's films of his works as he is for the books themselves, and film is one of the places that offers a long history of medievalism. Medieval subjects appear in early silent films and continue today. But what makes a movie "medieval"? Probably it takes place in the Middle Ages or tells a medieval story, such as Kevin Reynold's *Tristan + Isolde* (2006) or a classic like Otto Preminger's *Saint Joan* (1957), although the story likely has some differences from the medieval original. Of course, there are some obviously non-medieval elements: the characters are speaking in contemporary language and have really nice teeth. Also, while the setting is often clearly "medieval," it may or may not echo the particular elements of the specific point at which the original text was written. For instance, Antoine Fuqua's 2004 *King*

Arthur takes place in 487 CE, a date closer to when the historical Arthur might have lived, but it does not remotely resemble the world of the medieval Arthurian romances from which it (loosely) draws its story. The attempt to "historicize" or "authenticate" the work by making Arthur a Romanized Celt leading a cavalry of Iranian Sarmatians means that the film departs vastly from any extant version of the story, whether chronicle or romance. Similar effects can be seen in Ridley Scott's *Robin Hood* (2010), starring Russell Crowe, in which Robin Hood, an archer in the English Army, reads letters from his stonemason father (who likely would not have been literate in the eleventh century): the French armies arrive in a scene that is essentially a medieval Omaha Beach; and Maid Marion fights in her father's place (the last has some precedent in medieval romance, but seems more inspired by Eowyn in Tolkien's *Two Towers*). Any sense of "history" or "authenticity" it attempts to provide is itself a fantasy. This sense of anachronistic time is parodied pointedly in *Monty Python and the Holy Grail*, which opens with the date "932 A.D." on the screen yet proceeds to offer obviously ruined castles and other elements of a medieval landscape enshrouded (sometimes literally) in an undemarcated "past," in which any specificity about the period is blurred, creating a fantasy Middle Ages in which steeds are actually coconuts clacked together, the post-Norman (1066) French are already inhabiting castles and making fun of the English, and Modern Historians (not to mention anarchosyndicalist communes) appear in the landscape.

In Robert Zemekis' *Beowulf* (2007), there is quite a bit of psychology driving the story, almost as if the film filters the Middle Ages through Freud, since the increasingly monstrous characters are all products of unions between the male characters and Angelina Jolie's Grendel's Mother, who might best be referred to as Monster Barbie. Obviously, this is not *Beowulf*, the eleventh-century Old English poem. In *A Knight's Tale*, the poor page and son of a roofer, William Thatcher, ultimately becomes a knight by impersonating one; as Ulrich Von Lichtenstein – who seems to be named after a medieval writer who told many lavish tales of tournaments and jousting for ladies' favor – his success at jousting wins him admiration, a lady, and eventually a title. His entourage begins with two fellow pages but they are quickly joined by Kate the Armorer who puts a Nike Swoosh on her products and Geoffrey

Chaucer, who spends half the movie naked because he repeatedly loses his clothes gambling. These figures are not quite medieval; nor is the repeated playing of Jock Jams at the tournaments (especially Queen's "We Will Rock You"), nor the various contemporary dance interpretations. Or are they?

In Chaucer's *Troilus and Criseyde* and Knight's Tale, or Chrétien de Troyes' *Cliges*, or the Alexander romances, or the Romans Antique, figures from the past appear looking decidedly like medieval knights and ladies, heroes and villains, engaging a similar kind of anachronism that these films do – even having classical figures reading medieval books and listening to medieval music (Criseyde, a Trojan, seems to be reading the twelfth-century Benoît de St. Maure's *Roman de Troie*, for instance). The characters and stories may be "medieval" in contemporary adaptations, but they can still act like modern people and work out contemporary problems, just as Chaucer's characters may be Trojans and Greeks, but the past becomes a place for Chaucer to work out his most medieval concerns about how romance and love operate, what constitutes appropriate masculine behavior, how war affects love, and how the future (readers of his story) will interpret the past he presents to them. This particularly literary relationship to the past, which brings the Middle Ages into the present through the injection of contemporary concerns and modern superficial details as a way of making it meaningful to a current audience, certainly finds its origin in medieval narrative. So if medieval movies (and other medieval forms such as novels, television shows, or video games) seem inherently anachronistic, that is actually when they are at their most medieval.

MEDIEVAL VIDEO GAMES

Although technology has marked our era as starkly different from that of the Middle Ages, it cannot seem to divest itself entirely of an infatuation with the past. Like fantasy stories that harken back to medieval worlds, video games often take the same approach to offer gamers a way to experience a world of magic, dragons, and swordplay without any of the risks – and without giving up the safety and security of having a bathroom nearby. Games such as *Dragon Age: Origins* (EA Games 2009), *Dante's Inferno* (EA Games

2010), and *Fire Emblem Awakening* (Nintendo 2013) bring gamers to a medieval world where they can wield swords, cast spells, battle monsters, and engage in the tactical art of strategic movement and archery while removing the "internal-combustion engine" and guns of other popular role-playing games (RPGs).

To emerge successful in the *Dragon Age* franchise, the player must be proficient in weaponry and warfare, defeating countless enemies along the way and killing the great dragon-esque Archdemon in the final battle. This closely parallels – at least superficially – the concerns of actual medieval texts where knights are judged on their prowess in battle (killing enemies and avoiding death themselves), though they leave out the deeper, symbolic motivations found in both the literature on which they base their environments and the literature written today that looks to the pre-modern world for setting and inspiration. There seldom appears to be a more intellectual message hidden in the hack-and-slash mode and the well-wrought storyline so loved by medieval video game connoisseurs – which is in no way meant to discredit the value or worth of the games themselves. After all, they do what they are supposed to do (offer gamers an escape from reality for a time), and they do it well. Particularly in the medieval fantasy genre, there is an added layer of fascination that brings a contemporary world not only to the crime-ridden streets of Los Angeles or New York but to a world and era where magic seems to fit seamlessly and where wielding a sword is the greatest test of strength – where the reality of the Middle Ages is itself an enchantment for the modern world.

MEDIEVAL NOVELS

If a contemporary novel is set in the Middle Ages, is it medieval? This is not a spurious question; while the novel itself clearly draws from the medieval romance (see Chapter 3) as one of its antecedents, as a genre it emerges well after the Middle Ages. In the now somewhat out-of-date *The Rise of the Novel*, Ian Watt acknowledges the classical and medieval antecedents of the novel but suggests that what ultimately separates them are realism and reading audience. The former, according to Watt, causes authors to attempt to represent a more detailed, circumstantial view of human existence, in which characters are more individuated, time takes on a more historical specificity, and spaces become increasingly concrete and specific. These, he says, create an "air of complete authenticity" (1957: 27), which the authors achieve through a "descriptive and denotative use of language" (1957: 29).

In *The Rise of the English Novel 1600–1740*, Michael McKeon offers a sense of the novel's audience as produced by the rise of printing, and he adds that reading skills were often more developed than writing, particularly among the lower classes and that the "necessary industrial mechanisms exist for a marked increase of reading of narrative by the lower orders" (McKeon 1987: 52). Although he is somewhat skeptical about identifying statistically a reading audience in the eighteenth century, he does offer that "Both authors and readers, we may assume, were profoundly affected by the epistemological revolution whose intricate and far-reaching ramifications [they choose to document]" (1987: 52). In McKeon's view, the novel has less of a distinctive break from the romance and exists on more of a continuum, but in any case it is not the same as a medieval narrative. One way to think about this change is that characters develop psychologies; this puts their interiors inside – unlike medieval narrative forms in which the interior is often made exterior. In a medieval narrative, a character's anxiety about self-identity may be projected on the obstacles he or she must overcome, whether those are the derision of the populace (often seen in hagiographies), a dragon or giant (often seen in romances), or the conquering of an enemy (often seen in epics). A character in a novel may meet with many obstacles, but what becomes important is how the character responds to those obstacles, and how these help form an identity. So what happens when novels are set in the Middle Ages, especially when they draw their subject matter from actual medieval narratives? The desire to use the new form to tell old stories begins fairly early on; Horace Walpole's *Castle of Otronto* (1764) is often considered the first gothic novel because of its medieval setting and fantastic, dark elements. Walpole himself was conscious of blending the "old" romance of the Middle Ages with the "new" romance of the novel, attempting a combination of two forms. As such, he may be said to be the first "medieval" novelist, but he is certainly not the last, and the Middle Ages – real or imagined – remains a popular setting in which to explore a variety of stories.

While Watt's observations about readership certainly characterize this body of work, reaching audiences of varying ages and kinds, his observations about realism are addressed complexly in these works. Novels set in fantastic worlds cannot be said to be realistic, and yet, the ways in which authors often describe those worlds, creating every detail of life, are modeled on the novel's method of employing realism. Novels attempting to create a more realistic Middle Ages end up providing levels of historical detail and observation never seen in a medieval romance. Characters' motivations, whether they are wizards like Merlin or dragon riders, peasants, crusaders, or queens, are often explained in psychological terms, and these tales make use of novelistic forms like the *bildungsroman*. Thus, the question asked above remains: if a novel takes advantage of all the developments of the post-medieval genre, but sets itself in a real or imagined real world, is the novel medieval?

Since Walpole, both high realism and high fantasy novels set in the past have become increasingly popular, as we've noted above. Beyond the examples discussed in the "Epic Fantasy" section of this chapter, prime examples include T.H. White's *Once and Future King* (1958) and Anne McCaffery's *Dragonriders of Pern* series (1971–6). There are stories for middle-grade children, like Lloyd Alexander's *Chronicles of Prydain* (1964–68); E.M. Koningsberg's *A Proud Taste for Scarlet and Miniver* (1973), which tells the story of Eleanor of Aquitaine in heaven awaiting her husband; and Karen Cushman's Newbery Award winning *Catherine, Called Birdy* (1994) about a young medieval English girl anxious about growing up. There are many medieval novels for young adults; a pair of series that show the dichotomy of fantasy and realism while telling nearly the same story are Michael Spradlin's *Youngest Templar* (2008–10), which tells the story of a young orphan employed by the Knights Templar, and Catherine Jinks' *Pagan's Crusade* (1993–2008), which replaces Spradlin's Holy Grail with bad smells and bad teeth. In the adult realm, series like Ken Follett's *Pillars of the Earth* (1989) about building a cathedral in a fictional town, and Marion Zimmer Bradley's *Mists of Avalon* (1982), which tells the Arthurian story from the women's points of view, engage a range of readers, again balancing a fantastic notion of medieval reality against an equally fantastic notion of medieval fantasy.

Medieval novels come in several forms: works that draw on medieval landscapes and themes, with knights, castles, and magic;

novels retelling or reexamining tales from medieval literature, especially Arthurian ones; novels that draw their background from medieval history, focusing on historical figures or events; and novels that tell invented medieval stories. What constitutes "medieval" in these works seems to be twofold. On the one hand, elements of fantasy often construct the text as medieval, whether the presence of magic rings and potions, or figures like Merlin or Tolkien's Gandalf, who represent a magical "lost" (sometimes even lost within the story) world. On the other hand, the "medieval" can be a kind of high realism that focuses on bad odors, poor hygiene, dung, lice, and the plague and other harsh details of an imagined medieval life. This is itself a kind of fantasy – not that there weren't bad teeth, bad smells, and terrible diseases in medieval life, but given that these are a background to existence, the relentless drawing attention to them is a modern fantasy of the medieval, since medieval literature draws little attention, if any, to these "realities" of medieval life. Put simply, if everyone has bad teeth, it is unlikely that anyone would notice to point it out. (In Anya Seton's *Katherine* [1954], about Katherine Swynford, the mistress of John of Gaunt, she creates what might be seen as a great moment of medieval realism, when someone notices that Katherine actually has good teeth – and all of them.) These two narrative impulses are not mutually exclusive; fantasy and realism can coexist within these stories as well. There are certainly examples of medieval novels that employ both an attention to what they perceive as the realities of life in the Middle Ages while still engaging various magical or fantastical elements.

Certainly these novels (and increasingly, graphic novels such as M.T. Anderson's version of Chrétien's *Yvain* [2017] or Seymour Chwast's *Dante's Divine Comedy* [2014]) draw from medieval antecedents in a variety of ways, often very productively. Lloyd Alexander's aforementioned *Chronicles of Prydain* take stories from the Celtic tradition, particularly the *Mabinogion*, and combine the Welsh legends with lively characters and contemporary personalities who face magical situations. The main character, Taran of Caer Dalben, a foundling tasked with caring for Henn Wenn the Oracular Pig, longs for adventure and excitement, rather than his mundane tasks at home, but by the end of the series, after many magical adventures, longs for home and quiet, which, of course, he cannot return to because he turns out to be the High King of Prydain. While these longings are certainly the same as those that drive Perceval in Chrétien's *Conte de Graal* or Wolfram van Essenbach's *Parsifal* (both thirteenth century), we do not get inside Perceval's head in the same way that contemporary stories do, drawing from the tradition of the novel which foregrounds interiority and psychology in ways that their medieval antecedents do not; although it's clear that these antecedents do establish a kind of story that writers still want to tell.

The medieval quest romance provides fruitful ground to tell stories of heroic development. The romance itself is the genre of individual development, which is why these stories translate so effectively into novels. In medieval romance, the hero – often, but not always a young knight – generally in search of something (a lady, or an object like the Holy Grail), travels through lands real and magical having adventures and finally achieving the goal. This external quest stands for interior development; for instance, in *Sir Gawain and the Green Knight*, the Green Knight's game becomes Gawain's adventure – to fulfill his promise he must traverse strange lands and fight strange creatures, all to discover the truth about himself. This journey of discovery is in a great deal of fiction, particularly young adult, drawing on the antecedent of the *bildungsroman*, or coming-of-age story; the protagonist's path from uncertainty to a greater self-knowledge, and a stronger sense of his or her social purpose combines both narrative traditions, romance and novel. By setting stories in the past, authors have recourse to more elements of fantasy (such as dragons, giants, castles, spells, and magicians) and to different worlds, which provide a clear outlet for heroic actions and behaviors.

What makes these modern tellings of medieval stories, authentic or imagined, compelling is the flexibility of the imagined Middle Ages, which can appear in many guises. Anne Eliot Crompton's *Sir Gawain and Lady Green* (2010) essentially re-narrates the story of *Sir Gawain and the Green Knight* from the point of view of the Green Knight – imagined as a beautiful woman named Gwynneth – making it her coming-of-age story. Catherine, in *Catherine, Called Birdy*, plays in dung and is engaged to a much older, violent man, while Pagan, in *Pagan's Crusade*, observes the repulsive demeanors and profound stinks of the Templars for whom he works, as

Kushman and Jinks attempt to make vivid a world of the past, yet their observations and their appeal as characters come from their seemingly modern desires – Pagan's for family and Catherine's for freedom. The Middle Ages, in these works, is a time of restrictions and limitations, which can nevertheless be transgressed. For authors like Bradley, the Middle Ages is a mystical and fantastical time in which to examine the roles and power of women in the Arthurian story, which seems often to consign them to the margins. Indeed, many medievalist novels do focus on the female characters and view the Middle Ages as an opportunity to construct various kinds of feminism – pagan, exceptional, and conventional.

As with the films, it is possible to locate what is most medieval in medievalist novels in what seems least medieval – their anachronism. Because all these works are written by modern authors for a modern audience, they engage the past through the present, and the intersection of the two is what lures an audience that may not be particularly engaged by the medieval originals – or they might be. Many scholars interested in the "real" Middle Ages are also engaged by medievalism, and for many, medievalism was the route they took to the Middle Ages. Finally, what the two "medieval" bodies of work (medieval and contemporary) share is a fascination with telling stories of the "past" in order to access the present. After all, as Chaucer sets the Wife of Bath's romance, "In th'olde dayes of the Kyng Arthour" (Chaucer 1987: CT III 857), which he says are "manye hundred yeres ago" (Chaucer 1987: CT III 863), so the medieval versions of Arthurian, classical, or historical stories are just as driven by anachronism as contemporary ones. What is medieval about medieval novels is their interest in using a distant past to examine issues in the present.

A reader would never mistake T.H. White for Chrétien de Troyes, but what about something like Seamus Heaney's popular translation of *Beowulf*? Considered by scholars to be a somewhat fanciful version driven by Heaney's own concerns, particularly his Irish background, the translation was praised for readability and accessibility, qualities which seemed, in the reviews of the translation, to make it more contemporary than medieval. That said, if *Beowulf*'s own readers found the poem accessible and readable (or listenable – and Heaney was lauded for his readings of the translation, as well as a recording), then is a translation that captures these features, privileging them over getting the specifics of Old English "right," ultimately more authentic in the experience it creates? And does the mere fact that we're accessing the poem in our own language make it more contemporary than medieval? Are all translations acts of medievalism? Maybe they are.

CONCLUSION

This whole realm of exploration of the use of the medieval in the present (or indeed, in any present after the Middle Ages can be said to have ended) is a field of study in itself. Medievalism, and its partner, neomedievalism (as the use of the medieval in popular culture is often called), seek to understand the long and continuous life of the Middle Ages. The goal of medievalism is not to compare present artifacts to their medieval antecedents and find them wanting, but to consider what it means that the Middle Ages remain so valuable for the present, which seems so superficially different from the past. Why do the Middle Ages continue to invade modernity, and what kinds of things can they mean and do in our own time? In what kinds of ways is the medieval used progressively, and in what kinds of ways can it be coopted for very regressive and dangerous purposes? A great deal has been written on this topic, whether focusing specifically on medieval literature (examinations of the Arthurian story, for example), on particular countries, on politics, on film, or on contemporary media. The current popularity of shows like *Game of Thrones* and *Vikings* and their parallels in other media show what a fruitful area of exploration medievalism can be.

Medievalism can also be dangerous; the Middle Ages have been "claimed" by white supremacist groups, neo-nazis, and the Ku Klux Klan as an imagined white, isolationist past ruled by values seemingly positive on the surface but with destructive and highly problematic undertones. As these groups are on the rise in Europe and North America, heed must be paid to the ways in which the Middle Ages get used in much darker ways than the examples we've discussed in this chapter. Medieval symbols have been appropriated by these groups to represent a repressive (at least, to anyone who doesn't fit their narrow definition of acceptable – women, non-whites, non-Christians, LGBTQIA, etc.) past ruled by exclusion and violence. Crusade language, which has closer connection to medieval literature than some of these other appropriations, has characterized the so-called War on Terror that has arisen after the September 11 terrorist attacks in the United States and has escalated on both sides, leading to Islamophobia in the West. Economic conditions have sometimes been described as leading to a New Feudalism, a version which enslaves its workers without any of the sense of symbiosis that characterized medieval feudalism. While these are not particularly literary expressions of medievalism, they deserve mention, and for those interested in this more troubling side of the field, there are some suggestions for further reading below.

Medievalism is many things, but at its center is a looking backward, whether very specifically to its predecessors, or through a series of interpretive or imagined lenses. One of the many things that medievalism can best do is bring readers back to its sources, to a study of the real Middle Ages and its texts. Medieval films, novels, and video games may offer an imagined going back in time, but engaging with medieval literature itself gets a lot closer to experiencing the eras of castles and knights. As readers, we can never remove the filter of our own history and knowledge, but to look at the medieval texts – either in their original languages or in translation – offers a rich experience of the origins of this tradition. It offers a looking glass into history as well as into the hearts and minds of readers as well; into the world of the twenty-first century that has emerged from the foundations of a medieval past.

FOR FURTHER READING

We have not recommended any primary texts for this section, as it seems likely that most readers have a good knowledge of medievalism and have encountered a variety of primary sources in their reading, viewing, and game-playing lives. For some good introductions to the subject, readers might consider starting with: *The Cambridge Companion to Medievalism*. **(2016). Ed. Louise D'Arcens. Cambridge: Cambridge University Press**, or **Tison Pugh and Angela Jane Weisl (2012).** *Medievalisms: Making the Past in the Present*. **London: Routledge**.

To approach medievalism more theoretically, readers will find great value in **Kathleen Biddick's (1998).** *The Shock of Mediev-alism.* **Durham, NC: Duke University Press**, and **Carolyn Dinshaw's (2012).** *How Soon is Now?: Medieval Texts, Amateur Readers, and the Queerness of Time.* **Durham, NC: Duke University Press**, which provide very thoughtful examinations of the period. If Tolkien paves your way into medievalism, **Tom Shippey's (2003)** *The Road to Middle Earth.* **Boston: Houghton, Mifflin**, and *Tolkien's Modern Middle Ages.* **(2008). Ed. Jane Chance and Alfred K. Siewers. New York: Palgrave Macmillan**, provide thoughtful examinations of his impact on medievalism and indeed, the study of the Middle Ages itself. For those interested in gaming, *Digital Gaming Reimagines the Middle Ages.* **(2013). Ed. Daniel T. Kline. London: Routledge**, offers a series of articles on specific games and their use of the medieval, while *The Medieval Hero on Screen: Representations from Beowulf to Buffy.* **(2004). Ed. Martha Driver and Sid Ray. Jefferson, NC: McFarland** is one example of the extensive bibliography of works on medieval movies. *The Middle Ages on Television: Critical Essays.* **(2015). Ed. Meriem Pagès and Karolyn Kinane. Jefferson, NC: McFarland** may be the only volume dedicated specifically to medievalism on the small screen. For those interested in the political side of medievalism, **Andrew B. R. Elliot's (2017).** *Medievalism, Politics, and Mass Media.* **Cambridge: D. S. Brewer**, and **Bruce Holsinger's (2007).** *Neomedievalism, Neoconservatism, and the War on Terror.* **Chicago: Prickly Paradigm Press** offer different takes on how the Middle Ages are finding new life on the contemporary stage, often in ways as frightening as they are enlightening. For a study of medievalism that isn't set in the Middle Ages, and might be called unconscious medievalism, consider **Angela Jane Weisl's (2003).** *The Persistence of Medievalism: Narrative Adventures in Contemporary Culture.* **New York: Palgrave Macmillan**.

For an overview of the development of medievalism and its history, consider: **Matthews, David. (2015).** *Medievalism: A Critical History.* **Cambridge: D. S. Brewer**.

Medievalism: Key Critical Terms. **(2014). Ed. Elizabeth Emery and Richard Utz. Cambridge: D. S. Brewer** offers a range of essays on the specific terminology that governs this particular study, and **Richard Utz's (2017)** *Medievalism: A Manifesto*. **Kalamazoo, MI: Arc Humanities** offers a different way of thinking about and using the Middle Ages for the future. The rich body of medievalism scholarship shows how considering the use of the past in the present is developing as a scholarly field adjunct to, but independent from, medieval literature itself.

HOW TO WIELD A SWORD IN THE MIDDLE AGES
THE LITERATURE OF WAR AND VIOLENCE

Perhaps you've been to *Medieval Times*, a popular culture destination in the United States that offers visitors an opportunity to see a live "medieval" tournament where knights in colorful tunics engage in combat with swords, maces, battle axes – sometimes on horseback, sometimes on foot – in order to defend or win the hand of the princess. Or perhaps you've seen a full-contact jousting tournament or watched the Battle of the Nations. Or perhaps you've seen a movie about the Middle Ages where knights went to war on behalf of their king, fighting in bloody fields with swords and shields until death or victory. Many current fantasies of the Middle Ages are built on violence – often a violence controlled by rules and elevated by values – but violence nonetheless. In that sense, current depictions have a great deal in common with their medieval antecedents; as Richard Kaeuper notes of medieval literature of war and tournament, "almost without fail these works give prominence to acts of disruptive violence and problems of control" (Kaeuper 1999: 22). War, while capable of bringing glory and triumph to individuals and communities, was also perpetually disruptive, no matter how just the cause or complete the victory. Tribal societies depicted in earlier medieval works such as *Beowulf* or the *Niebelungenlied* are entrenched in conflict and warfare in ways that seem inescapable while the texts simultaneously comment on how destructive these impulses are to any kind of social harmony. The epics and *chansons de geste* valorize military prowess but are never able to escape the losses that conflict brings to the community. Conversely, however "wrong" the enemy may be, their skill can bring a grudging sort of admiration and respect, even in the face of their wholesale defeat.

While fascination with knighthood might seem to originate as a contemporary phenomenon looking back on the past, authors and poets in the Middle Ages were equally fascinated with the mechanics and ideals of knighthood and warfare and exploring how those two realms intersected. Knights, in medieval literature, become the warriors about whom adventures are written, the "ideal" in a world questioning its values, trying to grapple with defining that ideal and exploring whether it ever truly could be attained, and asking if the precepts of chivalry – which served as a code of conduct governing a knight's behavior and influenced medieval warfare (at least for the noble classes) – function in reality or exist merely as an ideal fantasy. Texts questioned the correlation between violence and masculinity, the intersection of pagan and Christian values in relation to war and revenge, and examined – sometimes in exquisite detail – the day-to-day life of Crusaders fighting under what they believed to be a divine mandate. Exploring ideals of behavior (both one's own and one's enemies') within problematic conflicts is a hallmark of this body of literature; while less frequent, one also sees an interest in tactics, weapons, and methodologies of fighting. Whether the conflicts within the texts are territorial, religious, or other, the literature always strikes a balance between the glorification of war and a questioning of its destructive effects – topics which continue to engage the interest of writers and filmmakers to this day. To trace the history of these engagements, read on and learn about what medieval texts have to say about wielding a sword in the Middle Ages.

CHIVALRY (WHICH IS NOT DEAD)

The word "chivalry" carries the echoes of *cheval, chevalier*, and *chevalerie*. Meaning, respectively, horse, knight (one who rides a horse), and horse soldiery, it identifies its practitioners as members of the nobility, as well as their status as *bellatores*, or fighters. Developed between c. 1170 and 1220, with influences from many earlier military groups, such as the Cavalry of the Holy Roman

Empire, Teutonic knights, and perhaps even the Moors, chivalry encodes values of bravery, honor, training, and service. As it developed, it continued to emphasize social and moral virtues as well as military ones; in *Sir Gawain and the Green Knight* (14th century), the pentangle on Sir Gawain's shield represents (among other things) the five chivalric values: piety, courtesy, chastity, fellowship, and generosity, showing that manners and virtue have come to outweigh the originary martial concerns. By the late Middle Ages, chivalry was as much a moral code as a military one, focusing equally on the warrior ethos, religious piety, and courtesy (which we will discuss at length in the next chapter), which worked together to establish a functional definition of nobility and honor for high-ranking knights.

Knighthood, as an institution, was comprised of vassals and liege lords who operated somewhere in the upper-middle of the feudal system between peasants and royalty, and often stood as a community's first line of defense against invaders and marauders. When a lord called upon his knights, he expected them to answer as the code of chivalry required: promptly, faithfully, and prepared to go into battle in the name of their liege. Feudalism stretched from the king down to the peasants who worked the land, with lords and vassals often holding dual roles. A knight is one such example: he might be lord of his own lands, commanding the loyalty of his own vassals, while being a vassal himself to a baron, marquis, or duke. All lords themselves were vassals to the king; when summoned to war by the crown, they would in turn muster their own knights to form the king's army.

And the chain of benefits did not only flow in one direction. Liege lords provided housing and food to their peasant vassals, along with protection from bandits, in return for their loyalty and labor. While a contemporary perspective might well decry that the rich exploited the poor during the Middle Ages, the medieval world understood feudalism as a way of life – a partnership between lords and vassals – that engaged with the complexities of social relationships in a wholly different way.

Common misconceptions about the Middle Ages often reduce the era to a barbaric time when peasants were forced to work the land under the cruel oversight of an exploitative lord. While some of these notions hold a degree of merit – laborers often did work under conditions that would not satisfy any current standards – they do not account for the ways in which feudalism was a symbiotic relationship. Peasants and laborers understood their way of life to be what Fortune had ordained for them. Although historical examples show this relationship to be heavily exploited and often brutal, the theory was that the lord would provide for those below him and ensure they had what they needed to survive and raise a family, an expectation that is lost in capitalistic systems. Knighthood, as an integral and crucial part of the feudalistic chain, theoretically guaranteed that lords and laborers would have equal protection in the event of an invasion or catastrophe. The extent to which this symbiosis actually functioned as it was designed is not the subject of this volume, and is rarely addressed in the literature; although warfare conscripted people from every level of society, the literature of war, chivalry, and conflict was for the most part concerned with the top, not the bottom, of the feudal triangle. However, the awareness of the destructiveness of war on human society, at least, resonated throughout the community. Because chivalry was reserved for male members of the first estate, its literature rarely speaks directly to anyone else, although there are several examples, such as Heldris de Cornuaille's *Roman de Silence* [The Romance of Silence] (13th century), in which women passing as men prove as chivalric and as fearsome on the battlefield as their male counterparts.

Geoffroi de Charny (1300–56), a medieval author who wrote *Le Livre de Chevalerie* [The Book of Chivalry] (1352), further classifies the various levels of knights (or men-at-arms as they are sometimes called). Considered to be himself the "quintessential knight of the age" (Kaeuper and Kennedy 1996: 3), Charny evaluates the several conditions of knights and gives an account of them, ranking them by their abilities and activities. He first considers those knights who simply pursue "recreational" jousting, to use a modern term. Such knights are those who, "if they hear of any festivities or other occasions for jousting... will be there if they can... [yet] neglect and abandon the other pursuits of arms" (Geoffroi de Charny 1996: 87). Those other pursuits include participation in local wars, whether it be to defend their kinsmen or to demonstrate their faith and loyalty to the rightful lord who is their liege. For Charny, these knights deserve the most praise, as they put their lives and lands at risk for the sake of others, emphasizing the mutual responsibility and unity inherent in the feudal system.

Knighthood as an institution, then, was founded largely upon a man's ability to perform well in feats of arms, either at the recreational level (which, at its core, was used to train knights for live combat) or, more importantly, at the level of actual warfare. Loyalty and obedience to one's liege was paramount, and, indeed, trust between lords and vassals was the glue that held the feudal system together. This system appears in countless pieces of medieval literature, from the epic to the romance, as authors considered the ways in which knighthood impacted the lives of nobles and commoners alike. Early texts such as *Beowulf*, set somewhere in the sixth century and estimated to have been written down anywhere between 800–1000 CE, show the origins of chivalry in the behavior of the *comitatus*, or war-band, while crusade literature such as *Richard Coer de Lion* [Richard the Lion-Hearted] (early 14th to late 15th century) and Joinville's crusade chronicles compare the ideals of knighthood between Christian and Muslim men-at-arms. Perhaps one of the strongest institutions of the Middle Ages, knighthood not only played an integral part in medieval politics, but also influenced the ways in which the medieval warrior understood his relationship to his lord, king, opponent, and even to his God.

Quite apart from the chivalric romance, which embodies these values in concert with the interests of courtesy and love, chivalry has its own body of literature, volumes which sought both to describe the code and instruct knights in its practice. Ramon Llull's *Book of the Order of Chivalry* (c. 1274–76), written in Catalan, was translated and disseminated throughout Europe and is foundational in contemporary understanding of medieval knighthood. At its heart a reformist work, his text attempts to convince crusader knights to regulate themselves and their behavior, thus keeping their focus on their true cause – to defeat the Saracens. Dividing chivalry into seven parts to represent the seven planets that put the terrestrial bodies in order,[1] Llull hopes that his exploration of chivalry, its origins and its workings, will put knighthood into order as well. His prologue begins with a squire seeking knighthood encountering an aged knight who has moved into the forest to live; after asking that the knight explain the Order of Chivalry to him, he is given the book itself, which allows him to understand nobility and honor as well as the structures he must learn to follow. Charged with bringing the book back to the court to "restore the devotion, the loyalty, and the Rule that the knight must observe in order to profess his Order" (Llull 2013: 38), the young squire brings the book to the King who allowed any knight who aspired to the order to make a copy. Llull, in a series of short sections, emphasizes a combination of secular and religious virtues that combine to make the perfect knight, one deserving of the honor that should be paid to him by all the people. A knight worthy of honor will be "loved, for he is good," … and "feared, for he is strong"; and must perform good deeds and provide counsel to his lord (Llull 2013: 80). Geoffroi de Charny's *Book of Chivalry* was likely influenced by Llull's, showing many similar values. Written to provide a guide to knighthood for Jean II of France's Company of the Star, chivalric behavior on Crusade was also his inspiration.

Less a guide than a biography, *L'histoire de Guillaume Marshal* [The History of William Marshal] written in the thirteenth century, provides a descriptive overview of a knight engaged in chivalric practice. William Marshal (c. 1147–1219) was a skilled tournament jouster and knight errant who received the title Earl of Pembroke through marriage. The biography describes the flower of chivalry and the ideal knight who embodied all the chivalric virtues. How much of this is exaggeration and embellishment is uncertain; however, the biography does provide a useful portrait of idealized chivalric behavior in war and in the court, as well as presenting a fascinating history of a man who served five English kings.

Despite the subject pertaining predominantly to men, writing about warfare and chivalry was not just the province of male authors and participants; c. 1410, Christine de Pizan wrote the *Book of Deeds of Arms and of Chivalry*, which among its explanations of military strategy and tactics, and explanations of medieval warfare technology, is one of the first sources of information about early gunpowder warfare and weaponry. Drawing on some of the assumptions of Vegetius' fourth-century *De Rei Militari* [Of Martial Kings] and the fourteenth-century *Arbre des batailles* [Tree of Battles] by Honoré Bouvet, Christine says that she writes "by true affection and a genuine desire for the welfare of noble men engaging in the profession of arms" (Christine, *Arms* 1999: 12). Although a woman writing a manual for warfare was unprecedented, Christine was well prepared for such a work, having discussed the importance of a knight's moral education in the *Epistre d'Othéa* (1399–1400) and the details and value of chivalry in her biography of Charles V. Christine valued moral education and skilled tactics over physical prowess, suggesting that true chivalry comes from "good fortune, good judgment, diligence, and strength" (1999: 4).

Covering details of military practice from how an army should be drawn up for combat to how fortresses should be equipped with water during a siege to what equipment is needed for an assault, Christine is nonetheless more interested in the moral questions raised by warfare and what constitutes acceptable moral practice, particularly issues of loyalty, service, expense, and obligation. Her sense of what is acceptable in war is driven by ideas of what constitutes a just war. Acknowledging that all war "involves killing and various other kinds of evil, things forbidden among Christians by God's law," she still acknowledges that some kinds of warfare are acceptable: those which "recover what is right," and "wars in defense of one's country when it is attacked." However, she suggests consulting the opinion of "competent jurists or lawyers" (1999: 152) to determine if other sorts of quarrels constitute just or unjust wars. Knights who serve in unjust wars, Christine asserts, "will go the way of perdition without great repentance" (1999: 153).

These works of chivalry are both fascinating in their own right and as an adjunct to much medieval courtly literature, whether concerned directly with war and violence, as are the works covered in this chapter, or with individual prowess, as is the courtly romance. While some medieval works, such as the Icelandic saga discussed below, seem to revel in unbridled violence, these works demonstrate that for many medieval knights, violence was often a highly considered, regulated, and ritualized behavior. Kaeuper (1999) observes that:

> however glorious and refined its literature, however elevated its ideals, however enduring its link with Western ideals of gentlemanliness – and whatever we think of that – we must not forget that knighthood was nourished on aggressive impulses, that it existed to use its shining armor and sharp-edged weaponry in acts of show and bloody violence.
>
> (Kaeuper, *Chivalry* 1999: 1)

Of course, those rituals and regulations, and even Christine's questions about the definitions of a just war, did not make the violence they justified any less destructive.

CHANSONS DE GESTE

The *chansons de geste* [Songs of Heroic Deeds], a group of French epic poems, emerge in the late-eleventh and early-twelfth centuries, the result of several centuries of oral transmission; although the genre continues into the fifteenth century, they achieve their apex between 1150–1250. Often called the "Matter of France," to distinguish them from the Arthurian "Matter of England," or the various classical narratives that made up the "Matter of Rome," they were primarily concerned with early French history, particularly that of the Carolingians and their descendants. The best-known examples are the *Chanson de Roland* [Song of Roland], which dates from c. 1080 and tells the story of Charlemagne's loss to the Saracens at Roncevalles (and the ultimate victory that follows), and *Guillaume d'Orange* (c. 1140), a cycle of poems dealing with William of Orange's various battles with and victories over the Saracens. The *chansons* are clearly concerned with myth-making; much is known about the historical Charlemagne, but the narrative version presents a somewhat different picture of a king concerned with chivalry and valor, given to great flights of emotion at the loss of treasured retainers and enormous anger in the face of defeat. Little is known about the historical William of Orange, but the poetic cycle creates a tale of a life of great exploits, starting in "glorious youth" and ending in a "saintly death" (Ferrante, Guillaume 1974: 1). Primarily concerned with feats of military prowess in which Christian heroes triumph over their pagan adversaries, or narratives of rebellious barons battling their kings or each other, the popularity of the genre seems to arise from the way that the older stories easily reflect the current situation at the time of writing, the struggles of the Capetian dynasty in France and the rise of the Crusades.

The *geste du roi*, the first cycle of poems of which the *Chanson de Roland* is a part, tell loosely related stories about Charlemagne's exploits. Another series, the *Doon de Mayence* (13th century) focuses on a group of stories related only by the theme of rebellion. These poems cover a variety of feuds: personal, familial, royal. As Joan Ferrante notes, these tales demonstrate that "pride that is quick to take offense and slow to forgive leads to self-perpetuating and often horrifying violence" (1974: 3), violence which the *chansons* both critique and glorify. While the *Chanson de Roland* revels in graphic descriptions of bodies split in half, brains squirting out of ears, and even horses cleaved to death, *Raoul de Cambrai* (12th or 13th century), one of the rebellion poems, shows how feuding can lead to the slaughter of innocent victims when a group of nuns is burned within their church.

In some sense, the different sub-genres may seem to critique each other; in *Guillaume d'Orange*, the weakness and often lack of generosity of the king does not lead to feuding – instead William and his loyal fellow knights turn their energies to fighting a common enemy. While strategically this allows the knights to gain fiefs by capturing them, since the king fails in his duty to provide them for his vassals, these alliances also serve a larger purpose. The loyalty of William's family and followers becomes a model by which the Christian corpora can be increased, as it leads converted pagans to join the fight (men) or the family (women). The conversion and subsequent marriage of pagan women to Christian men then complements, and to an extent, offsets, the violent slaughter of the pagan enemy.

THE SIEGE OF JERUSALEM

Particularly violent is the Middle English *Siege of Jerusalem* (c. 1370–80), an alliterative poem that survives in nine manuscripts. The poem focuses not on the Siege of Jerusalem during the first Crusade in 1099, but on the siege by the Romans in 70 CE, which is portrayed as divine retribution enacted by the Roman emperors Vespasian and Titus for the death of Jesus Christ. Ralph Hanna famously called the poem "the chocolate-covered tarantula of the alliterative movement," and noted that the poem received almost no critique because it was "so offensive as to exist on the suppressed margins of critical attention" (Hanna, Siege 1992: 109). The poem has received more critical attention recently, in part because of its racism and xenophobia, and this has revealed the poem's intensely sadistic and violent nature, as well as its virulent anti-Semitism.

The text seems to revel in gory and graphic detail, such as a Jewish woman eating her own child during the siege, or the slaughter of the temple priests. Some have read the poem as questioning, if not critical of, such anti-Semitism in its seeming sympathy for the everyday citizens of Jerusalem and its meditations on whether war is ever justified. That said, the poem nonetheless seems to exploit a fascination with violence; like a contemporary horror film, the *Siege* seems to treat its graphic content as essential to telling a good story. Like many of the *chansons de geste*, the *Siege* seems to use past events to echo and justify present sentiments during the years of crusade, and to suggest the depth of Christian anxiety about practitioners of other religions.

LITERATURE OF THE CRUSADES

The Crusades are, perhaps, the most well-known – and misconstrued – wars of the Middle Ages. To this day, they continue to permeate popular culture through film, literature, drama, and even appear in contemporary political discourse particularly as it relates to terrorism, often without primary evidence to support their depiction. Even during the Middle Ages, authors found interest in the so-called "holy wars" that lasted two hundred years or more, depending on the source. The beginning of the Crusades is uncontested, marked by the declaration of Pope Urban II at the Council of Clermont in 1095. His speech remains one of the most influential in creating the martial history of the Middle Ages, as he inspired medieval Christians to go to war against the Seljuk Turks who barred Christian pilgrims from entering Jerusalem. It also focused anti-Saracen and anti-Semitic rhetoric on a specific cause. Seven campaigns would follow his, until 1291 when the last European crusader castle fell in the city of Acre (which lies on the northern coast of present-day Israel, and whose crusader city has recently been unearthed by archeologists). Afterwards, there were various other "crusades" throughout Europe, though none of them took place in the Holy Lands.

Geoffrey de Villehardouin (1160–1213) chronicled his experience in the Fourth Crusade, offering a primary source for understanding the inner workings of the Crusades from the necessity for monetary funding to the infighting between various groups and divergent allegiances. His *Chronicles* also provide an account of the capture of Constantinople and of the fire that destroyed much of the city after a conflict arose between the Greek natives and the Latin conquerors during what was supposed to be a stopover on the way to reconquer Jerusalem. This conflict became the driving force of the Fourth Crusade, in which Crusaders fought not against Muslims in the Holy Land but against fellow Christians who held the "gateway" city of Constantinople. Despite the overload of information found in Villehardouin's text, it still manages to provide a story of intrigue and war, of betrayal and suspense, of decapitation and misadventure, and even of royal marriage.

Villehardouin's chronicle certainly wasn't the only text to offer a first-hand account of the Crusades. Jean de Joinville (c. 1224–1317), in his *Histoire de Saint-Louis* [History of Saint Louis] (1309), gives detailed depictions of the Seventh Crusade as he and King Louis IX set out together in 1248 on an expedition to Egypt where the Crusaders planned to attack Syria. When the army was captured, Joinville and the king were ransomed together and became friends. Joinville became seneschal of Champagne upon their return to France but refused to accompany the king on a crusade to Tunis (1270) (which would prove fatal for Louis). Joinville's crowning work, the *Histoire*, was commissioned by Jeanne of Champagne and Navarre, wife of King Phillip the Fair, and was presented – after her death – to her son, Louis X. The heart of the work is its lengthy central account of the crusade, bordered by descriptions of Louis's early life and of his later reign, death, and canonization. However adulatory of Louis himself, Joinville does not hesitate to criticize the second crusade on which the King embarks; he not only tells of financial difficulties and wastefulness, dangerous sea voyages, and the ravages of disease, but he also critiques the crusading army for confusion and lack of discipline, giving a first-hand view of the miseries of the crusade experience.

In addition to the historical accounts, fictional narratives inspired by the Crusades and the popular figures who rose to fame because of them also emerged during the Middle Ages. *Richard Coer de Lion* is one such text, written by an unknown author and surviving in texts dating from the early-fourteenth to late-fifteenth centuries. It recounts the adventures of King Richard the Lion-Hearted and freely inserts moments of fiction into an otherwise historical account of King Richard's participation in the Third Crusade. Exhibiting elements of a *chanson de geste*, the poem reimagines the biographical platform of Joinville and Villehardouin's works and explores the ways in which fantasy and history can be intertwined. Some of the notable fictions in the account include an incident in which King Richard falls ill – and is only revived after being fed the flesh of a young Saracen – and the use of a revolutionary siege weapon: the beehive, combining both entertainment and history and contributing to the valorization of King Richard I.

The "Pagan Cause is Wrong, the Christian Right," the line from the *Chanson de Roland* which might be used to sum up some of the attitudes distributed among the *chanson de geste*, crusade chronicles, and crusader romances is, of course, highly xenophobic, although the sense that it is possible for someone to be assumed into the Christian corpora by means of conversion suggests potential reconciliation, though that is hardly an antidote to the texts' fundamental racism. While some crusade materials would suggest a wholehearted endorsement of these values, many others are more skeptical and questioning; grudging admiration for Saladin as a leader – particularly as a merciful one who let the citizenry of Jerusalem leave the city freely and allowed all Christians to be affordably ransomed – and respect for Saracen military techniques often informed discussions of these events, as did anxiety about the purpose and cost of the Crusades themselves. Joinville's *Life of St. Louis* is particularly concerned with the expense and destruction wrought by the Crusades, feeling that they also harm the King's reputation among his people, but he is not alone in interrogating the problems of war and violence; the very unitary cry of Charlemagne's armies is not ultimately as representative of Christian attitudes as it seems.

Of course, the European view is not the only one represented in medieval literature. The Arabic material on the Frankish wars, as they named these conflicts, shares a great deal with the opposition. Amin Maalouf's *Crusades Through Arab Eyes* compiles a variety of texts – chronicles, histories, and documents – showing a similar nexus of self-justification, religious conviction, occupation with prowess and military superiority, and some grudging respect for the other side's occasional martial success. Maalouf quotes Saladin as saying "Regard the Franj! [the Franks, or Europeans] Behold with what obstinacy they fight for their religion, while we, the Muslims, show no enthusiasm for waging holy war" (Maalouf 1984: 1), suggesting a significant difference between the two sides. However, once the chronicles begin the narration of specific conflicts, they often describe and praise various Franj siege engines and tactics for the difficulty in overcoming them. There is also equal description of the strategies and tactics of their own armies, including the use of *naptha*, or Greek Fire. Attitudes towards correct behavior in war might seem familiar to readers of the Western texts; for instance, Kamāl al-Dīn says: "Ilghazi made his emirs swear they would fight bravely, that they would hold their positions, that they would not retreat, and that they would give their lives for the *jihād*" (1984: 93). These chivalric attitudes are similar to those fostered by Charlemagne in Roland, Oliver, and the rest of his troops in the *Chanson*. Salāh al-Dīn (Saladin) weeps at the loss of his troops and other injustices of war as much as Charlemagne does, and he is idealized as much as any of the Western military leaders for both his battlefield prowess and his post-battle generosity to people on both sides.

Equally, the Arab texts applaud the end of the conflict. Maalouf quotes Abu'l-Fidā as saying:

> After the conquest of Acre, God struck fear into the hearts of those Franj still remaining on the Syrian coast. Thus did they precipitately evacuate... the sultan therefore had the good fortune, shared by none other, of easily conquering all those strongholds, which he immediately had dismantled.
>
> (Maalouf 1984: 259)

He adds: "Thus were the Franj, who had once nearly conquered Damascus, Egypt, and many other lands, expelled from all of Syria and the coastal zones. God Grant that they never set foot there again!" (1984: 259). If these works are not fictionalized in the same way as the European examples, they still provide the same fodder for examining shared views of conflict and violence.

EPIC

Not all medieval literature of war and violence is chivalric in its impulses, nor does it all deal with conflicts between Christians and pagan enemies. Medieval epics draw from classical traditions that begin with *Gilgamesh*, and share many of their characteristics. An epic can be defined as:

> a poem that is (a) a long narrative about a serious subject, (b) told in an elevated style of language, (c) focused on the exploits of a hero or demi-god who represents the cultural values of a race, nation, or religious group (d) in which the hero's success or failure will determine the fate of that people or nation. Usually, the epic has (e) a vast setting; it covers a wide geographic area, (f) it contains superhuman feats of strength or military prowess, and gods or supernatural beings frequently take part in the action. The poem begins with (g) the invocation of a muse to inspire the poet and, (h) the narrative starts *in medias res* ... (i) The epic contains long catalogs of heroes or important characters, focusing on highborn kings and great warriors rather than peasants and commoners.
>
> (Wheeler 2017)

Medieval epics are motivated by these same traditions, whatever their specific relationship to the classical epic may be; *Beowulf*, an Old English poem with earlier, oral Scandinavian origins, clearly exemplifies many of these qualities as fully as the *Iliad* and the *Odyssey* do, although uncovering any overt relationship between the classical poems and the *Beowulf* author is patently impossible.

Certainly, *Beowulf* satisfies many (if not all) of the conditions outlined above, retelling the feats of a great warrior as he fights to rid the land of not only one, but several fearsome monsters, culminating with his own death at the hands (or talons?) of a greedy dragon (though not without first dealing a fatal blow to his adversary). The story, first told as an oral narrative and later transcribed, considers a culture constantly immersed in war and surrounded by enemies on all sides. The setting of the tale predates the arrival of Christianity to Britain; though, as Margaret E. Goldsmith observes, "we have every reason to believe that the poet and his audience were grounded in the Christian faith and accustomed to listen to Christian poetry" (1962: 75).

As a result, the Christian overtones that appear within the text seem to grapple with the pagan themes of the narrative, introducing a tension that produces the question of how a reader is to interpret

Hrothgar's statement, for example, that Beowulf's killing of Grendel was achieved through the power of God. Goldsmith asks whether the "general maxims about life [peppered throughout a story of fabulous adventures]... are necessary to the poem, or whether the author, or someone else, has scattered them broadcast, in order to lend an odor of sanctity to what might otherwise smack of heathenism" (1962: 72). Does one simply dissociate these intrusions from the original narrative and understand them as coming from the background of the scribe? Can there truly be an "original" version of the tale when the "original" version itself surely evolved and expanded with each oral retelling? Or has the version that survives in the extant manuscript become the "true" version, memorialized and immortalized as it was written by the poet? Or perhaps it is simply, as Goldsmith suggests, that the author "was concerned with the hearts and minds of men... and only secondarily with wars and banquets and feats of swimming" (1962: 72), giving the poem a subtly different emphasis – perhaps – than what its oral narrators originally intended.

Certainly, the text praises the warrior victorious in battle, but it also considers the dangers of sending the King – who is both the head of the war-band (also known as the *comitatus*) as well as the representative of the whole community and its health – into the lion's (dragon's) den. A king must be fearsome in battle, but *Beowulf* considers the consequences of a king's recklessness, putting not only his own body in harm's way but the body of his nation as well. At a time when the hierarchy of tribal government was based more on prowess than on lineage, the death of a king left the nation in a dangerous state of disarray, caused, in part – or even mostly – by feuding between tribes.

Another integral part of the narrative – found often in the medieval epic – is battle: Beowulf fights with Grendel, Grendel's mother, and even the dragon. Combat becomes so important to the text (and to the authors writing these epics) that even the swords become characters. Hrunting, a sword given to Beowulf by Unferth, is described as a treasure, hardened by battle. Despite this, though, it fails Beowulf in his fight with Grendel's mother. He must use another sword, one forged by the giants of old, to behead the monster, suggesting perhaps the failure of human means to defeat the supernatural.

In actual warfare, too, the failure of weaponry was a legitimate concern. A knight's sword was more than just a piece of steel: it represented his honor, his prowess, his ability to uphold his duties as a man of arms. In film and theater, swordplay is often dramatized and romanticized: the clash of steel rings out across the battlefield, sparks fly, the villain and hero fight for countless minutes with neither's sword going dull until finally one strikes a fatal blow.

In reality, swordfights lasted seconds, not minutes, and parries were more often made with a shield or the flat of the blade rather than the edge. Edge-on-edge parrying would quickly dent and ruin a sword no matter how well-crafted (and it certainly did happen, as evidenced by the medieval swords found in museums with triangular wedges missing along the blade), though different styles required different battle strategies. Ordinarily worn on the hip, the size, style, and shape of the blade varied depending upon the geographic origin. Broadswords (likely the sword described in *Beowulf*) and claymores (large and typically ranging from thirty to forty inches in length) as well as longswords and hand-and-a-half swords predominantly accompanied European knights while the falchion was often found in the Middle East. The katana was the sword of choice for the Japanese Samurai, and was designed to slash an opponent immediately from the draw (hence the famous curvature of the blade).

In addition to swords, other weapons in medieval warfare include spears (also known as halberds or pikes), bows and arrows (which could be either short or long, the longbow gaining fame in the English Battle of Agincourt [1415], or mechanical [in the form of a crossbow in which the string was mechanically wound back and released by way of a trigger mechanism rather than by hand]). The battle axe, in some cases, also made its way into the hands of combatants and makes its appearance as the weapon of choice for the Green Knight in *Sir Gawain and the Green Knight*.

Although the monsters in the text – Grendel, Grendel's mother, the dragon – certainly offer their own measure of death and destruction, the narrative also considers the ways in which humanity can be its own worst enemy. In the end, the hero of the tale – Beowulf – fails. He dies at the hands of the dragon, perhaps because of his own hubris, thinking he was invincible. His followers are left prophesying the ultimate destruction of the Geats at the hands of the Swedes, just as the downfall of Heorot – because of internecine conflict after Hrothgar's death – was predicted earlier in the poem. Thus, readers and listeners of the medieval epic discover a story that is as elegiac as it is triumphant.

Found in the same manuscript as *Beowulf*, *Judith* (c. 975–1025) reveals that medieval epic heroes were not exclusively male. The text recounts the beheading of the Assyrian general Holofernes by the Israelite Judith of Bethulia, a retelling of the Book of Judith, a deuterocanonical biblical text still found in Catholic and Eastern Orthodox bibles, in the Protestant Apocrypha, and in Jewish non-biblical sacred collections. Although incomplete, the poem tells of a heroic woman grounded in virtue and blameless in the eyes of her people who triumphs over the monstrous Holofernes, beheading him in his bedchamber after he falls into a drunken slumber and leading the Hebrew army to victory. The descriptions in *Judith*, and in particular the descriptions of Judith herself, echo those found in *Beowulf*, foregrounding their shared traditions, despite very disparate sources.

The *Nibelungenlied* is another epic text that considers the role of women and even begins with a comment about ancient tales and how they describe the feats of great heroes, their victories and, in some cases, their tragic deaths. Written in Middle High German c. 1200 by an unknown author, the text has its own dragon whose blood offers the power of invincibility to any who bathe in it. At the heart of the narrative lies a feat of arms in which Siegfried must best Brunhild (a woman) in battle so that he may in turn win the hand of Kriemhild in marriage. He succeeds, but through trickery, using a cloak that makes him invisible. Nevertheless, Brunhild marries King Gunther, Siegfried's liege, and Siegfried marries Kriemhild. After time passes and quarrels ensue, the characters destroy each other for their trickery and deceit. Brunhild learns that it was not Gunther who defeated her, but Siegfried, causing her much grief. Hagen kills Siegfried because of this, after learning of the one spot where he remained vulnerable (where a leaf prevented the dragon's blood from touching him), and Kriemhild mourns for many years. She eventually goes to Hungary to marry another and invites her brothers to her lands. Intent on revenge, Kriemhild has the Burgundians massacred, beheads her brother Gunther, and kills Hagen with Siegfried's sword before getting her own head cut off at the hands of Hildebrand. A version of this story is told in the Icelandic *Volsunga Saga* (13th century).

Although the text, at its surface, may appear to be a brutal narrative, it presents a reality often faced by medieval nations. It warns against the dangers of unbridled vengeance and the use of tactics that would circumvent the hallowed rules of chivalry. As attested by the varied and conflicting scholarly interpretations of the text, it offers a tale that does not have a simple "right" or simple "wrong." Katherine DeVane Brown looks at the different versions of the surviving manuscripts and analyzes the ways in which they appear to shift blame toward or away from Hagen for taking the actions he did. She particularly focuses on the B manuscript and the ways in which its presentation of loyalty – a major component in the success of feudalism – may have resonated with medieval audiences (Brown 2015: 356).

She ultimately concludes that, "Rather than simply caricaturing Hagen as a villain, the *Nibelungenlied* poet is able to preserve aspects of the traditional image of Hagen and present him as a generally wise and brave vassal whose initially misplaced loyalty causes him to act unjustly towards Siegfried" and that "Through this skillful adaptation of the courtly rivalry motif, the poet is able to present a new perspective on the problem of loyalty conflict" (Brown 2015: 377). Perhaps that is what all medieval epics, at a foundational level, attempt to do: consider social questions and issues and inject them into complex narratives that simultaneously problematize long-held beliefs while reaffirming the need for certain codes of conduct that promote peace, security, and survival for peasants and nobles alike.

Other examples of medieval epics include the twelfth-century French *Roman de Brut* [Story of Brutus] and *Roman de Rou* [Story of Rollo] by Wace, and the thirteenth-century English version of the *Brut* by Layamon; the Middle High German anonymous poem *Kudrun* (13th century), which shares many features and some characters with the *Niebelungenlied*; and the Spanish *Cantar de Mio Cid*, or *El Cid* [Song of my Cid], also from the thirteenth century. Dante's *Divine Comedy* can also be said to be an epic, and the form continues to shed influence on a great deal of the medieval period's literature, even if the poems themselves fit into other categories.

ICELANDIC SAGAS

One significantly different example of the literature of violence in the Middle Ages is the Icelandic saga. Written down in Old Norse in the fourteenth and fifteenth centuries, and drawn from extensive oral antecedents and events that took place primarily in the ninth to eleventh centuries surrounding the founding and colonization of Iceland, the sagas are stories of people (real and imagined; contemporary and historical), events (such as the colonization of Greenland and the discovery of Vinland), and places (such as the Orkneys or Western Iceland) linked to prominent families, and sometimes include mythological elements. These texts incorporate a great deal of violence, feud, and conflict as dynasties establish themselves. Like the feuds in *Beowulf*, which as noted above is likely a Scandinavian import into England in some oral form, the sagas show profoundly the extent to which violence is a part of medieval history.

For instance, *Egils Saga Skallagrim Sonar* [The Saga of Egil, son of Skallagrim] (earliest manuscript fragment, c. 1240) tells the story of Egil, son of Skallagrim, a farmer, Viking, and poet, whose life seems violent at every turn. At a young age, he kills a fellow child whom he believes to be cheating at games; he has continuous conflict with King Eric Bloodaxe of Norway, maintains various feuds with rival chieftains in Iceland, goes on Viking raids throughout the narrative, serves King Athelstan of England in battles against his fellow Vikings, causes a farmer to choke to death on his own vomit when he refuses to serve Egil his best wine, and finally, at the end of his life, desires to throw his silver onto the ground at the Althing for the pleasure of watching his fellow farmers fight over it.

What is striking in the sagas is not the violence per se, but that it plays out against a backdrop of other stories. Rather than being foregrounded, as it is in the *chansons de geste* which take as their subject armed conflicts and battles, the violence here takes place against a series of other narratives, with which the texts are primarily concerned, about the establishment of families in particular places. More than other examples, these works show the extent to which violence is part of the fabric of society, since it becomes part of a larger story rather than the center of the story itself. Many of the sagas are ultimately foundational narratives about the establishment of Scandinavian society in Iceland, the Orkney Islands, Greenland – even the attempts in Vinland and Markland in North America – as well as telling the stories of the families and communities associated with particular places such as the *Erebygga* [the Saga of the People of Eyri] or *Laxardalr* [The Laxdæla Saga] – but the sagas reveal how deeply conflict is a part of these histories. Although Iceland established a parliamentary system built on laws governing ownership, property, land use, access to resources, and the Althing (an annual governmental meeting that meted out punishments for abrogating these laws), it did not stop armed conflict from being very much a part of the social fabric.

CONCLUSION

Whether bloody and violent or detailed and instructive, texts about warfare and battles in the Middle Ages evoke a particular ethos, commenting on the ways in which a culture, community, or social class engages in violence for sport or survival. Narratives question what it means to fight a "just war," often wondering about the Crusades' economic, social, and moral position, and how the precepts of chivalry play into a knight's actions in battle. Medieval authors seemed equally concerned with factual representation – such as those who penned the crusade narratives, striving to relay details and events as they occurred so that readers might better understand the machinations behind long and heated conflicts – as they were with engaging fantasy to understand violence and social stability. Monsters become representations of human horror – and sometimes vice versa – blurring the distinction between unimaginable atrocity and the routine of medieval combat.

Where Beowulf battles dragons and giants, the raiders of the *Siege of Jerusalem* must confront the horror they reap themselves, becoming, perhaps, the true monsters of the story even if the author did not originally write them as such. Understanding medieval literature, then, sometimes requires both acknowledging the perspective from which it was written as well as seeing how it might be interpreted in a modern setting. Authorial intent, according to some critical theories, evaporates as soon as the manuscript leaves the hands of the writer; particularly in medieval literature, where texts often have no known author, it can play an even lesser role.

Nevertheless, people in the Middle Ages surely experienced violence and horror that today would be relegated to the movie theater. For all their reveling in violent detail, celebrating of chivalry and martial prowess, and glorification of military victories, the narratives and tales that emerge as a result are imbued with a sense of suffering and questioning, of wondering how or why such things must happen and how to move beyond the bloodshed to create something greater.

FOR FURTHER READING

PRIMARY TEXTS

As can be seen from this chapter, the literature of war and conflict in the Middle Ages is extensive and varied. For those interested in reading about chivalry from those who invented it and articulated its principles, see: **Geoffroi de Charny. (2005).** *A Knight's Own Book of Chivalry*. **Introduction by Richard Kaeuper, Trans. Elspeth Kennedy. Philadelphia: University of Pennsylvania Press; Raymond Lull. (2013).** *The Book of the Order Of Chivalry*. **Trans. Noel Fallows. Woodbridge, Boydell Press**; or **Christine de Pizan. (1998).** *The Book of Arms and of Chivalry*. **Ed. Charity Canon Willard. Trans. Sumner Willard. State College, PA: Penn State University Press**. Christine de Pizan, writing at the end of the period, both reflects how chivalry has changed as well as showing how a woman writes about a set of regulations that control the behavior of the men with whom she interacts.

For those interested in reading the literature itself, these five works, each from a different language and tradition, offer a broad view of how medieval writers viewed war and violence. While *Beowulf*. **(2001). Trans. Seamus Heaney. New York: W. W. Norton** might be the best known, and *Egil's Saga*. **(2004). Trans. Leifur Ericsson and Bernard Scudder. London: Penguin**, the least, they both offer a sense of a tribal society so driven by conflict that it is a feature of everyday life. A similar understanding of violence underlies *The Niebelungenlied*. **(2004). Trans. Arthur Hatto. London: Penguin**. Coming later in the period, *The Poem of the Cid*. **(1985). Trans. Rita Hamilton. London: Penguin** and

The Song of Roland. (2015). Trans. Glynn S. Burgess. London: Penguin, show a stronger influence of chivalry than the previous works and demonstrate the ways in which war is both a part of the existence of medieval knights and how destructive it can be. Taking that sense of realism one step further, the *Chronicles of the Crusades by Jean de Joinville, Geoffroi de Villehardouin* (2009), Trans. Margaret Shaw. London: Penguin offers a first-hand view of the Crusades from the European side, while Amin Maalouf's (1984). *The Crusades Through Arab Eyes*. Trans John Rothschild. New York: Schocken Books compiles a series of Arabic works that tell the same story from the other side.

SECONDARY SOURCES

For those interested in an historical view of the impulses, activities, and values that governed medieval knighthood, there are several resources available. David Crouch's (2005). *Tournament*. London and New York: Palgrave Macmillan provides an historical overview of the details of the tournament, while two works by Richard Kaeuper examine the function of chivalry, notably (1999). *Chivalry and Violence in Medieval Europe*. Oxford: Oxford University Press and *Medieval Chivalry*. (2016). Cambridge: Cambridge Medieval Textbooks. Medieval war, though often depicted in films as large groups of knights riding at each other hacking each other to pieces, is shown to be more complexly strategized and theorized in Helen Nicholson's (2003). *Medieval Warfare: Theory and Practice of War in Europe from 300–1500*. London: Macmillan. The specifics of the Crusades are considered in Hans Eberhard Meyer's (1992). *The Crusades*. Trans. John Gillingham. Oxford: Oxford University Press and Peter Partner's (1997). *God of Battles: Holy Wars of Christianity and Islam*. Princeton, NJ: Princeton University Press, with the second offering both a European and Islamic perspective. For those who find themselves compelled by the Icelandic saga, Jesse Byock's (1982). *Feud in the Icelandic Saga*. Berkeley, CA: University of California Press offers a comprehensive look at the way in which the narratives are driven by this particular variety of conflict. And for those who find this chapter heavily masculine and want to explore another perspective on medieval violence,

***Violence Against Women in Medieval Texts*. Ed. Anna Roberts. (1998). Gainsville, FL: University of Florida Press**, shows through a series of essays how women experienced and understood varying kinds of conflict, abuse, and destruction.

NOTE

1 In medieval cosmology, the earth stood fixed at the center of the universe, surrounded by the spheres of the planets, fixed stars, and *primum mobile* (prime mover, or God). The planets were therefore the Moon, Mercury, Venus, Mars, the Sun, Jupiter, and Saturn. The three remaining planets, Uranus, Neptune, and Pluto, had not yet been discovered.

CHIVALRY IS NOT DEAD
THE LITERATURE OF LOVE AND DESIRE

Harlequin Desire, an imprint of Harlequin Publishers, the largest publisher of romance novels in North America, offers the following guidelines for writers of modern romance:

> Powerful, passionate and provocative contemporary romances set against a backdrop of wealth, privilege and glamour
>
> - Intense, dramatic storylines with a highly sensual, passionate feel
> - Classic romance hooks mixed with juicy, unique elements
> - High-stakes conflicts (emotional and/or external) drive the plot
> - Every story includes the sense of a bigger world – extended families, corporations, brotherhoods, best friends, partners, secret societies
> - Sexual language is euphemistic and romantic, not explicit
> - The reader should feel swept away from the everyday
> - Characters should have believable, sympathetic motivations
> - An emotional payoff befitting a powerful, passionate and provocative read.
>
>   (Harlequin Desire Romance Writers Guidelines 2016)

When contemporary readers think "romance," these Harlequin Writers Guidelines may be what they imagine. From mass-market fiction to RomComs, romance has come to be the genre of love and desire, with a heavy tendency towards fantasy and formula.

Modern readers may have these same expectations when first diving into a medieval romance, and they will not be disappointed – they will certainly find emotional content and conflict, euphemistic sexual language, love triangles, and juicy elements including dragons, giants, and secret *rendezvous*. That said, modern readers should also be aware of certain differences. The resolutions of the stories may not be as neat as those found in contemporary romance – sometimes because the stories do not actually end due to manuscript loss, and sometimes because medieval authors were less interested in the conclusion than they were in the process. The obstacles facing the protagonists are as much internal as external, and the outer conflicts are often there to represent the inner struggles the knight faces as he embarks on his quest for both the lady and the honor and glory of chivalry. Indeed, some medieval romance sets the love plot aside entirely – or at least makes it secondary to this knightly development – and instead finds meaning in a religious resolution. Modern readers may find themselves asking, "Where's the love story?" And yet, for all that, the romance – along with the lyric and the fabliau – remains the genre of desire. That desire, however, may take on different forms than those with which the modern reader is familiar.

The phrase "Chivalry is not dead," often heard these days, acknowledges both the medieval romance's antecedents in the epic and its fascination with manners and courtesy; it has been suggested that the romance, medieval literature's most popular genre, was born from the intersection of the lyric and the epic, drawing the subject matter from one and the form from the other. The rise of the troubadour lyric and its descendants in France, Germany, Italy, and England (11th to 13th century) develops a sophisticated language and philosophy of love, which then finds its narrative expression in the romance – the genre of the quest in search of the fully realized self. While "romance" originally referred to the language in which the text was written – the vernacular rather than Latin – the name has come to refer to works dealing with the adventures of knights in a courtly society, preoccupied equally with prowess (deeds in battle) and courtesy (deeds in love). In the romance, these two impulses are frequently in conflict with each other, as are those of duty and desire – the duty of the knight to his king and country, and the desire of the knight for his lady.

Although the protagonists are generally those knights, in the romance, the lady gains more status and voice than she had in the literature of war. Although ultimately the genre remained about men, women acquired a great deal of narrative space in the genre because as sources of desire, they commanded tremendous power. The romance heroine, because of the expectations of courtly love, could (generally metaphorically) save her lover from death or consign him to misery. Although the genre's drive towards marriage ultimately constrained women's authority and voice, in the liminal space opened up by the romance plot, it allowed a wider range of self-expression, power, and subjectivity than other genres. From heroines who control both the knight's desire and the purse-strings to queens who gain control over the knight's death or life, from women who heal medically and emotionally to those who demonstrate great intellectual capability to women who pass as men and then become the heroes of the romance as well as its heroines, the genre is a rewarding place to investigate the potential of women in the medieval literary imagination. Of course, a great deal of this power is constructed within the sexual economy and is therefore based on a lady's desirability, and as a result is somewhat narrow; those systems of power primarily constrain the heroines. Other women in the romance can be seen wielding other types of authority, as the romances show a variety of women in roles other than as the beloved.

The romance tradition spread across medieval Europe, with versions of the same story (such as *Floris and Blancheflor* or *Tristan and Isolde*) often appearing in Old French and Old Norse, Middle High German and Welsh, Middle English, and Spanish. While many major authors, such as Marie de France (c. 1160–1215) and Chrétien de Troyes (c. 1160–91), developed this genre, its popularity is attested to in both the large number of anonymous and vernacular romances and the fabliaux which parody them with significant lewd energy.

The themes of troubadour love poetry are enacted within a narrative context that focuses on an individual and (generally) his adventures in pursuit of love. This focus puts the lead character's private, interior life in opposition to his or her (mostly his) public, exterior one. Romance style is "elastic and mobile," built with "hypotactically rich periodic syntax and consecutive constructions"

(Auerbach 1953: 128) and focuses on the mores and ideals of feudal knighthood, the fixed and isolated setting, the importance of women, and the idealized, fairy-tale atmosphere preserved primarily in *avanture* (Auerbach 1953: 131–3), arranged in a structure "characterized by the order and connection of events organized around the fiction of the love service, designed to represent a kind of unreality" (Auerbach 1953: 141).

Patricia Parker calls romance a form that "simultaneously quests for and postpones a particular end, objective, or object... which necessitates the projection of an Other, a *projet* which comes to an end when the Other reveals his identity or name" (Parker 1979: 4). The desired and postponed ending of romance often becomes a kind of textual obsession with conclusion, a need to wrap up the main story in a way that often values conclusion over clarity. This is the antecedent of the "and they lived happily ever after" of the Fairy Tale, the neat wrapping up that defines modern romance. In the medieval antecedents, however, whether the story ends happily (often with marriage, or revelation of the desired object) or unhappily (with multiple deaths), the texts always seem to drive towards a conclusion without always reaching it – the conclusion becomes secondary to the central body of the text, which is generally where most of the interest in the works lies. Endings are often problematic, pieced together, or inconclusive; romance remains "on the threshold before the promised end, still in the wilderness of wandering" (Parker 1979: 4), and the "focus may be less on arrival or completion than on the strategy of delay" (Parker 1979: 5).

Indeed, it's in the endings that modern and medieval romance most diverge; contemporary romance is always driven by a desire to tie up all loose ends, while medieval romance, as Parker notes, does not. She calls romance "inescapable" because of its tendency to enclose itself; romances frequently take place in liminal worlds that lie outside the texts' "real" world, which often feature enclosed spaces – the *locus amoenus* or place of love in which the revelation or consummation takes place – surrounded by threatening and dangerous oppositions. In these spaces forbidden loves can flourish, rules and regulations can be turned upside down, and magical creatures and peoples can roam freely. These spaces are called liminal because of the ways in which they blend the real and unreal worlds, and courtly figures often move seamlessly between them, as in Chaucer's Wife of Bath's Tale, where the knight can be in the real world of conflicting opinion in one line and see fairies dancing in the next, can meet with "A fouler wight ther may no man devyse" [a fouler creature no one could imagine] (Chaucer 1987: III 1000) and discover that she has the answer to his "real-world" problem.

Romance often takes place in liminal space, a transitional door-way between one world and another, a threshold between states in which rules are bent and expectations altered, in which transfor-mation and identity development take place. Corinne Saunders explores the forest as the archetypal landscape of medieval romance, a landscape that highlights "the conflict between social responsibility and individual passion," a "landscape of conversion and miracle" that "becomes a powerful symbol of the human need for regeneration," and a landscape that "extends far beyond its obvious associations with darkness and danger, incorporating themes of adventure, love, and spiritual vision" (Saunders 1993: xi). To put it simply, romance is the genre in which all sorts of crazy things take place – in order to work out complex interior and public problems.

Courtly romance emerges in the twelfth century as the medieval world is beginning to take shape, shifting from the tribal associations we see in *Beowulf* into the feudal system of manors and courts. A more stable and structured society produces more opportunities for leisure and entertainment, and the genre emerges as a result of these circumstances. George Duby suggests that the fixation on love arises from a need to control young, heavily armed men in groups; without the perpetual imminence of war, groups of retai-ners could cause a great deal of trouble. Love was viewed as a civilizing force, breeding good manners and behavior, and fetishizing the female in a structure that elevated her and made the desiring male vulnerable and passive (Duby 1992: 251). He views the romance as a narrative arising from the subject of the troubadour lyric. The values and assumptions of these foundational texts of love and courtesy (both the lyric and the romance) are put forward by Andreas Capellanus in the *Ars de Honesti Amandi* [The Art of Courtly Love] (1184–86), a series of lovers' dialogues accompanied by a list of the "Rules" of courtly love, which include "Marriage is no real excuse for not loving," "every act of a lover ends in the thought of his beloved," and "a man who is vexed by too much passion usually does not love" (Capellanus 1941: 185–6). For all that Capellanus calls these "Rules," they are more descriptive of how love and courtesy are understood in the lyric and romance tradition than they are a code of regulations; no courtly lover carried a laminated card with Capellanus' maxims tucked into his armor. The romance's literary genealogy is the combination of the lyric and the epic; the emotional content and context of lyric poetry, melded with the narrative drive of the epic, create the most popular secular literature of the Middle Ages.

MARIE DE FRANCE AND CHRÉTIEN DE TROYES

The first two key names in the rise of romance are Marie de France and Chrétien de Troyes. Marie de France appears to have written in England, Chrétien in France, both during the 1160s. Eugene Vinaver argues, based on Marie and Chrétien's works, that the romance's internal workings are inseparable from what we think of as literature (the private, one-on-one relationship of text and audience); the romance, then, is the first "modern" and "literary" genre (Vinaver 1971: vii). He sees a more decisive break with the epic tradition, from nationalistic to individualistic concerns (Vinaver 1971: 1). Robert Hanning echoes this assumption, noting that the romance's goal is the exploration of the depth and possibilities for the individual as subject (Hanning 1977: 3). Love is the subject of romance because it is a purely personal and individual endeavor. Adventure is a challenge of social values that offers "an alternative to identity defined by forces outside the self" (Hanning 1977: 3). The reader then engages in both the hero's struggle and his or her own as both a participant in the hero's quest and a member of the external world which seeks to define the hero through social expectation. The reader is thus integrated in a complex way that is impossible in the entirely public world of the epic or the solipsistic confines of the lyric.

Historically, the romance is an expansion of the short *lais* from the Breton tradition that Marie de France translates/creates/invents and the longer, more developed forms that Chrétien produces. While many are Arthurian, many are not. Romances fall into three primary forms: tragic (like the story of *Tristan and Isolde*), comic

(*Cligès*), and fantastic (*Bel Inconnu*). Romances are also often organized by "Matter," loosely defined as national content. The "Matter of Rome" explored the deeds of heroes from the Graeco-Roman tradition – the Trojan War, Alexander the Great, Thebes, and mythological figures, most often drawn from Ovid. The "Matter of France" included stories based on Charlemagne, Roland, and others of his knights, while the "Matter of England" focused on stories such as Guy of Warwick, King Athelstan, and King Horn. Most prominent among them, however, was the "Matter of Britain," the stories of Arthur and the Knights of the Round Table. While all of these "matters" transcended national and linguistic boundaries – there are stories about Roland in Spanish and about Orpheus in English – the Arthurian romance has the broadest spread and the greatest variation of forms, appearing in languages as diverse as Middle Dutch (e.g., the c. 1350 *Roman van Walewein*) and Old Norse (the 1226 *Tristrams saga ok Ísöndar*). The thirteenth century saw the rise of the encyclopedic, "vulgate" romances, prose works attempting to capture the entire Arthurian story; the *Lancelot-Grail* cycle included stories of Lancelot's upbringing and arrival at Camelot, the Quest for the Holy Grail, Merlin, and the Death of Arthur, while Malory's *Morte Darthur* (1485) essentially reproduces the form in English. In addition to these "matters," romances can have classical sources (*Sir Orfeo* [c. 1330]), draw upon historical impulses if not exact sources (*Flores y Blancaflor* [c. 1290] or *Layla and Majnun* by Nazami Ganjavi [12th century]), call upon allegorical dream visions (*Le Roman de La Rose* [1230/1275]), or derive from fantastic invention (*the Roman de Silence* [13th century]; *Aucassin et Nicolette* [12th century]; *Grisel y Mirrabella* [c. 1470–77]).

Romances found an audience among men and women of the upper classes, who were interested in seeing "stories in which their own ideals and anxieties were reflected" (Krueger 2000: 3). While the texts often praise and emulate courtly values, from their earliest iterations – such as in Chrétien's *Yvain* (1170s) – romances are not hesitant to interrogate those values and those who hold them. The courtly romance often holds a mirror up to its own society and finds it – if not wanting – at least worthy of critique. Marie de France's eponymous hero of "Bisclavret," (late 12th century) who becomes a werewolf and runs around naked, proves himself to be more human and loyal than any of the humans in the story, while the heroine of Jean D'Arras's *Melusine* (1392–94), who turns into a snake from the waist down on Saturdays, and who later becomes a dragon, embodies the genealogical and political values of the text better than her husband or any of the humans who misunderstand her.

The popularity of romance may, in part, come from its elasticity. Drawing from a vast network of sources and values, and telling a wide range of stories, historical and fantastical, romances captured the medieval literary imagination more than any other form. Their ability to speak to problems inherent in courtly society, to engage with issues both religious and secular, to bring stories about the past into the present, accounted for their spread; while their exploration of the individual's place in society; the function of good and evil, loyalty and responsibility; and their interest in love, honor, prowess, and duty accounts for their endurance. As Roberta Krueger notes in her introduction to the *Cambridge Companion to Medieval Romance*, "the great questions posed by romance – about personal and social identity, love and honor, good and evil – were neither resolved nor... supplanted" (2000: 5) as the Middle Ages shifted to the Early Modern period. Medieval romances may have first appeared in the twelfth century, but they are still appearing today.

This chapter's title, and much of what has been discussed here, considers romance's link to the present; however, to fully understand medieval (secular) literature of love, the origins of romance – and its commentary – must also be taken into account.

ROMANS ANTIQUES

The *Romans Antiques* or *Romans d'Antiquité* are a series of metrical narratives derived from classical sources that offer a mid-point between the more-epic *chansons de geste* (see Chapter 2) and the fully developed courtly romance. The *Roman d'Eneas* (12th century), *Roman de Thebes* (c. 1150–55), and Benoît de Sainte-Maure's *Roman de Troie* (1155–60) do not merely retell Virgil's *Aeneid*, Statius' *Thebiad*, or the Trojan War story, but alter the focus so that the texts offer both mirrors for princes and reflections on courtly love. For instance, the *Roman d'Eneas* is deeply concerned with Aeneas' love relationships with Dido and Lavine, the former a sign of his lust and distraction from his duty, and the latter an inspiration to him in his battle with Turnus. Benoît's *Roman de Troie* makes central the Trojan prince Troilus' love for the traitor Calkas' daughter, and his refocusing of the narrative becomes an inspiration for Boccaccio, Chaucer, Henryson, and Shakespeare as they retell the story of love within war.

A characteristic of this particular variety of the romance is its sense of being part of a tradition; Barbara Nolan suggests that each author "clearly had before him manuscript copies of Latin books, whose ancient, canonical matter he intended to collage, translate, or pillage for the sake of his particular public's pleasure and instruction" (Nolan 1992: 6). Therefore, for all the invention to be found in them, the genealogy of these texts shows a closer relationship to classical material than their Arthurian and Courtly cousins, although like all forms of romance, they remain somewhat slippery and hard to define. This genre can consist primarily of the three works discussed here, but it can also include Boccaccio's *Filostrato* and *Teseida*, Chaucer's *Troilus and Criseyde* and the Knight's Tale, and some might even say – although it's hardly a romance – Dante's *Divine Comedy*. Nolan suggests that this is a purely medieval, and perhaps Renaissance, genre, without contemporary examples (1992: 7), but perhaps films like *Alexander* and *Troy* (both 2004), by telling classical stories in a contemporary mode, could also be considered examples of this tradition.

THE LYRIC

Some of the earliest medieval lyric poetry can be found in the jarchas (also sometimes spelled kharchas) – poems from Southern Spain. The word itself comes from the Arabic word for "final," and indeed, these poems were the last words of the *muwashashah*, an Arabic poetic form that began appearing in the ninth and tenth centuries in the Middle East. *Muwashshahs* appear in both Hebrew and Arabic; these poems were highly structured and followed strict poetic forms, in part because they, like the troubadour lyrics that they influenced, were intended to be sung. The *muwashahahs* concluded with a jarcha, often written in the vernacular with Arabic elements; these concluding poems, particularly those found in Al-Andalus, or Islamic Spain, generally celebrate and explore love. They are generally constructed as direct quotations from one of the main characters in the longer poem, although many of the jarchas can be found in multiple *muwashshahahs*. Some are anonymous, but others are by well-known poets such as the Hebrew poet Yehudah HaLevi (1075–1141). In Spain, many of the poems are in the voices of women, and while their authors are anonymous, they remain an early lyric attempt to express women's experience in love, particularly the loss of love and grief that follows.

There is much dispute among scholars about their origins, as well as their influence on other medieval lyric traditions. While some argue that there is a direct connection between the jarchas and the troubadour lyric, others suggest that these are coterminous but primarily separate traditions. Concerning the Ibero-Romance jarchas, some have argued that these begin as Spanish poems that then find new homes attached to the longer Arabic and Hebrew narratives. In either case, these poems are some of the earliest extant vernacular love poetry in the Middle Ages and share with the tradition many themes, forms, characters, and assumptions, in particular, the primacy of desire (requited, unrequited, abandoned, fulfilled) as a subject for poetry.

William IX, Duke of Aquitaine and Potiers (1071–1172), despite a fairly extensive ducal career that included excommunication and divorce, is best known as being the first troubadour, or lyric poet, writing in Occitan (also Provençal), the vernacular language of Provençe. Likely inspired by Arabic and Hebrew poetry that came to Provençe through Southern Spain, the troubadour poems showed mastery of language, content, and form. William's biography, or *vida* describes him as follows:

> The Count of Poitiers was one of the most courtly men in the world and one of the greatest enchanters of ladies. He was a good knight at arms, abundant in his womanizing, and a fine composer and singer of songs. He went about the world for a long time, seducing women.
>
> (Chabaneau [trans. Weisl] 1855: 12).

His eleven surviving songs often deal with these exact themes (and it is likely the *vida* was written based on the songs themselves rather than his actual life). Troubadour poetry dealt with many themes, including war and politics, but it is best known as an emerging poetics of courtly love, exploring themes including unrequited desire, loss, jealousy, and the vulnerability of the lover, often in conjunction with an anxiety about the use of the vernacular; the poet's relationship to his language, material, and audience often paralleled the lover's relationship to the beloved.

Troubadour poems were philosophical and parodic, intellectual and humorous, emotional and vulgar – they were also, in a sense, formulaic, appearing in a variety of set forms, meters, and genres. The *canso*, or song, was certainly the most popular in its ability to express the widest range of ideas, but *tensos*, or debate poems, often between two or more voices, explored many ideas about love and many of the surviving poems by the *trobairiz*, or women troubadours, take this form. The *alba*, or dawn song, expressed great sorrow at the beginning of the day which separated the lover from his beloved, while the *servientes*, or songs of service, were used to consider knightly political relationships, as well as for parodies. The *pastorela* – poems about knights' encounters with shepherdesses – were often humorous (although sometimes violent and salacious) putdowns in which the poet's desires are cleverly deflected by a seemingly wiser peasant.

The poetry is often classified into three forms: the *trobar leu* (light) – easily accessible and often humorous poems; *trobar ric* (rich) – characterized by complex poetic forms such as the sestina, and practiced by Arnaut Daniel (1180–1200), Dante's favorite troubadour; and *trobar clus* (closed) – a style characterized by obscurity and complexity, explored deeply by Marcabru (1130–50), but ultimately destined to die out because of its inaccessibility. Reading these poems today feels, even in translation, like reading another language with a system of references and meanings that don't quite make sense; written for an elite audience that was "in the know," it spoke very selectively then as well.

These poetic forms spread widely and quickly, to the *Troveres* in France, the *Minnesang* poets in Germany, the authors of the *romancero* in Spain, the Gallician-Portuguese tradition of the *cantigas de amigo*, and to the *dolce stil novo* (a form named by Dante Alighieri) poets in Italy, among other places. Of course, each of these bodies has its own distinct poetic features and subject matter, yet they all express profoundly literary, elevated poetics of desire, characterized by complex metaphors, images, and symbols through which human emotion and the manipulation of language into art become deeply intertwined. These specific schools of poetry seem to lose steam in the fourteenth century during the Black Death, but love poetry certainly never stops being written, and many of the forms, conventions, ideas, and metaphors of the troubadours and their compatriots can be found in the work of the Elizabethan sonneteers and all the poets of desire who follow them to this day.

Francesco Petrarca (1304–74), although an ambiguous figure for the Middle Ages, as he is often claimed by the Renaissance and is credited with inventing the term "Dark Ages," was particularly vital in the development of the sonnet and the preservation of lyric love poetry; his *Rime Sparse* (Scattered Rhymes) all focused on his love for the beautiful Laura, a woman with whom he apparently had no personal contact but who became his poetic muse. His poetry, while often psychologically observant, relies heavily on the traditions of love poetry developed by the troubadours. Laura causes him infinite joy in her presence, but also despair because of her unattainability; she inspires him and his poetry, but he cannot reach her, nor can he reconcile his desires with his Christian beliefs. The lady as goddess which he recreates in his verse is very much the lady of the troubadours' unattainable love: an inspiration and an aspiration, but never truly someone knowable to the poet. Petrarch is certainly not the end of a tradition; perhaps it is better to suggest that he is transitional, as later poets, such as Thomas Wyatt, translate and recreate Petrarch in their own works, even as their ladies-on-pedestals become objects of skepticism as well as obsession.

BRETON LAIS

The genre termed by scholars as the Breton *lai* is best known because of author Marie de France, who in the twelfth century wrote in French but lived in England. Marie states that her purpose is to preserve the *lais* she had heard; she says, "I undertook to assemble these *lais* / to compose and recount them in rhyme" to bring these oral tales of adventure to a wider audience (Marie de France, trans. Hanning and Ferrante, 1978: 29). The twelve *lais* attributed to her in the Harley 978 manuscript (located in the

British Library, written in England in the mid-13th century, and signed by Marie) are: "Guigemar," "Equitan," "Le Fresne," "Bisclavret," "Lanval," "Deus Amanz," "Yonec," "Laustic," "Milun," "Chaitivel," and "Eliduc," all of which consider courtly life in some way and cater to an aristocratic audience, exploring chivalry and courtly love in their characters and situations.

The popularity of the Breton *lai* flourished more precisely between 1170 and 1250, along with other short narratives such as the fabliaux, though the exact criteria for defining the genre eludes modern critics. A.C. Baugh offers the following: to determine whether or not a particular short romance should be labelled as a Breton *lai*, one must consider if the text calls itself one; if it takes place in Brittany; references Brittany in some way; or retells one of the stories found among the *lais* of Marie de France (Baugh 1967: 196). Other scholars believe the *lai* to simply be a subgenre of romance, comparing the two as one might compare the short story to a novel. However, Matilda Tomaryn Bruckner argues that "the adventures narrated in the *lais* differ from those of romance: there is no quest; and personal experiences lead to private fulfillment and happiness, with no special relationship between the protagonists' destiny and that of society" (Bruckner 1999: 205). Internal referents within the texts also label the stories as *contes* and *gestes*, suggesting that the Middle Ages were not as concerned with the need for generic codification as scholarship today.

Examples of Middle English *lais* include *Sir Orfeo*, *Sir Degaré*, *Lai le Freine*, *Erle of Tolous*, *Emaré*, *Sir Gowther*, and *Sir Launfal*, which were composed sometime between the late-thirteenth or early-fourteenth and early-fifteenth century. Only two of those – Thomas Chestre's *Sir Launfal* and the anonymous *Lai le Freine* – are translations or adaptations of Marie's poems. Geoffrey Chaucer also penned his own Breton *lai* (The Franklin's Tale), and it is commonly agreed that he not only knew but made use of the Auchinlek manuscript which contains three of the early *lais* (*Lai le Freine*, *Sir Orfeo*, and *Sir Degaré*). Scholars disagree on his motive or purpose for writing such a tale. Some believe he was capitalizing on a trend and exploiting the sentimental nostalgia such a genre could invoke. Others, such as Kathryn Hume, assert that there is simply an appeal found within the magical ethos associated with the Breton tradition.

COURTLY ROMANCE

While the Breton *lais* are the most fluid of the romance narratives, the Arthurian romance tales are perhaps the most well-known and most prolific. Here is a brief overview of the narrative in its most condensed form:

Arthur is known as the son of King Uther Pendragon who, with the aid of Merlin the sorcerer, takes the guise of Gorlois and lies with Igerna, his wife, impregnating her. Gorlois is killed in battle, and Uther takes Igerna as his own. The tales variously diverge at this point, with Geoffrey of Monmouth's history claiming that Arthur immediately succeeded his father as king when Uther dies of an illness. Other versions of the narrative say that when his father became ill, Arthur was taken away as a baby to protect him against enemies who would wish him harm. Only when he returns to pull the fabled sword Excalibur from the stone does he reclaim his rightful place as king. These later tales, known as the Vulgate Cycle (or Lancelot-Grail Cycle [1210–30] – *Lancelot, Quest de Sant Graal, Le Morte Artu, Estoire de Merlin*) add to the Monmouth narratives, expanding the legends, adding new characters, and introducing new adventures. The narratives, as can be assumed by their name, focus heavily on Lancelot's character, from his birth in a lake to his knighting at King Arthur's court and the adventures that follow, to his love and longing for Queen Guinevere. The cycle also develops narrative branches that lead to the incorporation of Chrétien's *Chevalier de la Charette* [Knight of the Cart] (c. 1175–81), the introduction of a Grail Quest with Galahad, son of Lancelot, and influence Thomas Malory's later *Morte Darthur*.

In these cycles, under Arthur's leadership, the land prospers; various fiefdoms are united, and people flock to his castle, Camelot. The bravest knights of the land pledge service to Arthur, including Lancelot, the best of them all. Lancelot faces a conflict between love and duty, though, as he finds himself enamored of Guinevere, Arthur's queen. Eventually, they sleep together, and Arthur discovers the infidelity. Distraught, he is seduced by his half-sister Morgana le Fay (who has taken the guise of Guinevere using the same spell Merlin had cast on Uther). Together, they beget a child who Morgana raises in secret while Arthur sends his knights to find the Holy Grail – the cup used by Jesus Christ at the Last Supper – to heal the land suffering under his poor leadership.

Perceval is the knight who finally finds the cup and returns with it to Camelot. Arthur drinks, regaining his health and restoring the land while Mordred, his child from Morgana, challenges him for the throne. During the battle, Arthur's forces prevail, aided by Lancelot who kills many Saxons, and the intervention of a wraith-like Merlin who convinces Morgana to dismantle her protection spells. Mordred manages to impale Arthur, though, while Arthur stabs him with Excalibur. Dying, Arthur commands Perceval to throw the sword into the nearby lake. Perceval returns in time to see the Fates sailing to Avalon with Arthur's body where legend proclaims he will recover from his wounds and one day return to rule Britain as the once and future king.

Chrétien de Troyes is thought to have inaugurated the genre and was perhaps immersed in courtly life himself, as suggested by the representations of chivalry and courtliness in his works. His *Le Conte du Graal* (c. 1135–90), though unfinished, began the legend of the Holy Grail and is preserved in more manuscripts than any of his other romances. Some issues that appear in the text include the contrast between worldly and spiritual chivalry; feudal allegiance; and, of course, Christian allegory.

In the prologue to his *Le Chevalier de la Charrette, ou, Lancelot*, Chrétien appears to attribute the content and subject matter of the story to his patron, Countess Marie de Champagne. While scholars have debated the meaning of this preface, it is largely conceded that it fingers in some way the legendary Arthurian narratives of Celtic origin as the source material for Chrétien's tale. And it is in Chrétien's first romance, *Eric et Enide* (c. 1170), that he establishes the Arthurian setting that will play a role in most, if not all, of his later works, a setting that will influence Thomas Malory's fifteenth-century *Le Morte Darthur*.

In it, Chrétien considers the division between courtly love and chivalry, juxtaposing them in scenes such as a beauty contest whose victor wins not by looks alone but by the strength of her knight who intimidates the competition. When Erec voices his objection to this system, the victorious lady's knight, Iders, fights him and loses. Arthur's court then becomes the liminal space to which Iders is sent as a defeated knight – both a locale from which courtly values emerge and also a place to which those who fail must return, subtly interlinking the two and suggesting that, perhaps, these values are not quite so perfect as the ideal court would imply.

Chrétien lays the groundwork for themes such as the conflict between a knight's chivalric duty in battle and his courtly duty to his lady. When combined with Chrétien's *Yvain, ou le Chevalier au Lion* [*Yvain, or, The Knight with the Lion*] – believed to be composed concurrently with *Lancelot* – the texts highlight this dangerous dilemma to the point where Lancelot and Yvain face devastating personal failure and become suicidal when disgraced as knights and lovers. The road to redemption is a long trek for these men, though it does lead, eventually, to some form of resolution.

The tension between chivalry and courtliness in particular reappears in the anonymous poem *Sir Gawain and the Green Knight* when Gawain must choose between the seduction of a gracious lady (who also happens to be his host's wife) and his duty to Sir Bertilak, his host. (The text is discussed in greater detail in Chapter 6). There are still other Middle English verse romances, primarily from the fourteenth and fifteenth centuries, that follow the Arthurian mode, such as *Gawain and Ywain; Sir Gawain and Dame Ragnell*; and *Sir Gawain and the Carl of Carlyle*, to name a few.

Other authors include Wolfram von Eschenbach (circa 1170 – after 1220), a renowned German poet who was a soldier as well. Picking up where Chrétien left off with *Perceval le Gallois, ou, Le Conte du Graal*, Wolfram's first major work of fiction finishes and expands what Chrétien began, giving nominal characters identities and families where Chrétien simply left them unnamed. His greatest change, though, comes with the addition of an overarching theme which he explains in his introduction. He declares that the leitmotif of his narrative will be *triuwe*, which can be defined as a capacity for loving in total selflessness and is epitomized by the love of God (Wynn 1994: 192). Indeed, the narrative's main quest comes from the Christian tradition of the Holy Grail, believed in some legends to be the cup from which Christ drank at the Last Supper – others suggest that it was the cup used to catch Christ's blood as he was crucified – though there is little reference to it in Wolfram's work.

Considered one of the most significant German authors at the end of the twelfth century, Hartmann von Aue is known both for

his variety of literary production and for his adaptations and interpretations of the works of Chrétien de Troyes, introducing what
would become the classical form of the Arthurian epic for future
German poets. As is the case with most authors of the period, little is
known about the life of Hartmann von Aue – and much of what is
gathered from his works comes with an array of interpretative difficulties (for instance, whether his description of his participation in a
Crusade should be taken literally or understood as a literary device).

In his own version and translation of *Erec et Enite*, Hartmann
names Chrétien as his source, though he takes his own liberties
with the material, introducing into German literature the bipartite
structure of his predecessor's Arthurian tales and spending much
effort in the second half of the work chastising the ways in which
Erec loses the repute that a courtly and chivalrous knight must
have. Erec must seek adventures to redeem himself from idleness
and earn in deed the honor and fame he so quickly and hollowly
achieved in the first segment of the text. This focus on redemption
is what scholars believe to be what most distinguishes Hartmann's
work from Chrétien's and gives the tale a moral that emphasizes the
need for one to recognize and acknowledge his or her responsi-
bilities to society, bridging the gap between an ideal courtly
romance and the realities of life in a medieval feudal system.

Geoffrey Chaucer also took advantage of the popularity of the
Arthurian tradition, using it in texts such as The Wife of Bath's
Tale and parodying it in fabliaux such as the Miller's, Reeve's,
Cook's, Shipman's, and Merchant's Tales. The Wife of Bath begins
her tale (after a lengthy prologue) by immediately invoking the
legend of Arthur. She says, "In th'olde dayes of the Kyng Arthour, /
Of which that Britons speken greet honour, / Al was this land
fulfild of fayerye" (Chaucer 1987: CT III 857–9). Chaucer
acknowledges the magic of the Arthurian legend by connecting it
with a land "filled with fairies" (more loosely understood as simply
supernatural creatures). He then uses the backdrop of courtly love
and chivalric duty to interrogate the power of women over men
and how justice in such a system might work. The tale questions
what it means to be truly courteous and offers a path to redemption for a rapist-knight that might not be as clear-cut as other
legends suggest. The resolution to the narrative can leave more
questions than it answers, just as many Arthurian tales can leave

readers wondering just where, exactly, these figures stand in relation to each other, to the feudal system, and even to God.

Straying from the Arthur story, although keeping his texts within its universe, Gottfried von Strassburg – another medieval German author – is most known for his major work *Tristan and Isolde* (c. 1210) of which eleven complete manuscripts exist. *Tristan and Isolde* was clearly a wide-ranging story in the Middle Ages with examples from many places in many languages; while Gottfried's version may be the most fully articulated, he builds on earlier versions, such as Beroul's *Tristan* (12th century), and his fellow German, Eilhart von Ogberge's *Tristrant* (12th century). Beroul and Eilhart survive only in fragments, as does the version that Gottfried names as his primary antecedent, Thomas of Brittany's French *Tristan* (1155–60). However, works like Marie de France's "Chevrefoil" and the Old Norse *Tristrams Saga ok Ísöndar* (1226) attest to the story's significant popularity. Often considered to be Wolfram von Eschenbach's counterpart, Gottfried considers the psychological motivations of people, which makes him a master of characterization. And while love has its role in *Tristan and Isolde*, it becomes much more than a simple plot device. The text considers the ways in which the quality of love can differ in various forms, as well as interrogating the relationships between love / society, and love / death.

In Gottfried's version of the story, the history of Tristan's parents opens the text, complete with their secret love and sexual rendezvous after Rivalin (Tristan's father) is seriously wounded in battle. Rivalin recovers, though his survival is short-lived. He dies during a renewed assault against King Mark's kingdom along with Blancheflor, though she manages to give birth to Tristan before dying herself. To protect the child from Morgan, King Mark's enemy, a couple faithful to Rivalin name the boy Tristan and raise him to be both chivalrous and skilled in the arts. Once mature, he makes his way unknowingly to the court of Mark, his uncle. After a series of adventures, he slays a dragon and wins the hand of Isolde of Ireland, claiming her for Mark to unite the two kingdoms.

However, during the voyage back to Cornwall, Tristan and Isolde inadvertently drink a love potion and subsequently indulge in the carnal pleasures that inevitably follow. Interpreters of the text use the potion to morally justify an otherwise adulterous transgression, though other critiques see the potion as symbolic of an already blossoming desire between the two: Tristan slew the dragon and deserves to enjoy the courtly rewards for this knightly act. Ultimately, whether he intended the potion as symbolic or not, Gottfried seems to portray the two as destined for each other.

Mark, through various informants, suspects Isolde's treachery and requires that she swear an oath to her innocence while holding a red-hot iron. On the day of the trial, she asks a pilgrim – Tristan in disguise – to help her from the boat when she stumbles and publicly falls into his (Tristan's) arms. She then swears that she has not lain with any man except her husband and the person into whose arms she just fell. Even though she passes the test, Mark soon sees that she loves Tristan more than she loves him and so banishes both. In their isolation, they live happily for a time, desiring nothing but the other's presence.

The secluded grotto where they stay suggests that such perfect love is comparable to the monastic life and the contemplative union with God. They are eventually discovered, though, with a naked sword between them as "proof" of their chastity. Mark believes it and invites them back, only to catch them sleeping together at court, which leads to a second exile. (NB: Gottfried's text ends here, and the story continues based on his source's version). Tristan meets another Isolde – Isolde Whitehands – and marries her, though he is still in love with the first Isolde. He does not consummate the marriage and, in another knightly battle, receives a poisoned wound via an arrow to the groin (a trope found in Marie de France as well) that can only be healed by true love's kiss. The original Isolde is sent for while Tristan remains on a ship with Isolde Whitehands. Out of jealousy, Isolde Whitehands tells Tristan that Isolde will not come, and he dies. When Isolde arrives and finds him dead she dies over his corpse, and they are buried together, perhaps inspiration for Shakespeare's *Romeo and Juliet*.

Although the deeds of Arthur and his knights have come to characterize the medieval romance, other courts offered various stories and adventures for medieval poets to explore. While the Matter of Rome, the Matter of Troy, and the Matter of France provided significant inspiration for these stories, many remain only very loosely connected – such as the second half of Chrétien de Troyes' *Cligès*, which, despite ties to both the Arthurian and

Alexandrian courts, sends its named protagonist on a fabulous quest that includes faked deaths, magical potions, and mystical towers and gardens, and which ultimately affects the life of either court very little. Similarly, the *Roman de Silence* may be vaguely "Arthurian" because of the late appearance of Merlin; however, its main story – a girl named Silence brought up as a boy to inherit her parents' lands after King Eban forbids women from acquiring property – is not an "Arthurian" theme.

While courtly love is at the heart of many of these romances, with examples as diverse as Renaut de Beaujeu's *Le Bel Inconnu* (c. 1180–1230) and its many versions and translations, *Amadis of Gaul* (14th century), *Sir Degaré* (14th century), and Chaucer's Franklin's Tale, others draw on courtly traditions but find their focus in monarchial history or genealogy. *Guillaume de Palerne* (1200) may have a love story within it, but its larger concerns are in restoring the correct monarchs of Palermo and Aragon, through the wisdom and devices of Alphonse, who has been turned into a werewolf by an evil queen in order to derail these lines of succession, while Jean D'Arras' *Melusine* (1392–4) relies on the discourses of courtly love to bring Melusine and Raimondin together. The greater concerns of this romance, though, are the founding and legitimizing of Poitou, and issues of genealogy and inheritance, of land and property, and of dangerous traits take precedence. Within this very landed text, however, the supernatural elements of romance take flight – Melusine herself is a fairy who is cursed to turn into a snake from the waist down every Saturday, and when the curse is not broken through Raimondin's failure to keep his promise never to look at her, she turns into that staple figure of romance, a dragon, and flies away.

Other poems may be primarily characterized as romances because of their form as much as their plots and characters; many romances, such as the Middle English *King Richard Coeur de Lion*, mid-thirteenth-century *King Horn*, and fourteenth-century *Athelston*, are stories of war and conquest, separated from the *Chanson de Geste* by their brevity and focus. Romances of Charlemagne and the Crusades are popular in much of Europe – versions of poems like *Flores and Blancheflor* appear in the Old Norse corpus for instance – and these frequently are essentially martial at their hearts, although they often deal with Christian/Saracen conflict and interchange, with the goal of expanding the Christian corpora. *King Richard*'s military exploits are exquisitely detailed in romance fashion, and the goal of his "quest" is the successful siege of Acre and the reacquisition of the Holy Land; it is easy to see that these narratives – those aforementioned and others like the *Siege of Jerusalem* (c. 1370–80) and *Sir Ferumbras* (c. 1380) – are inspired by the same understanding of romance that drives the Quest for the Holy Grail narratives. The poetics of desire can be directed at land and expansion as much as at lovers and objects, and the questions of prowess and courtesy, of duty and desire, can be enacted within these more military narratives as well. While not *Romans Antiques*, these poems show that making any hard distinctions between varieties of the romance is a quest doomed to failure, as the webs of influence, cross-pollination, and intersection affect the romance more than any kind of categorization and compartmentalization can. These distinctions may be useful as a way of thinking about the genealogy of the genre, but they prove less helpful than understandings of how these texts merge and blend.

FABLIAUX

Sometimes the best route to understanding a genre is through parody. While the fabliau does not exclusively parody the romance, it certainly pokes fun at its lofty ideals of love. A short comic tale in verse, usually obscene and often scatological, the fabliau concerns itself with sexual activity detached from the higher ideals of courtly love. Filled with puns, allusions, jokes, tricks, ribaldry, lusty peasants, naughty friars and nuns, and cuckolded husbands, in the fabliau, to adapt the words of E. Talbot Donaldson on Chaucer's Miller's Tale, all the conventions of "romance degenerate into the complacent targets of a lewd whistle" (1970: 25). The fabliau appeared in France in the twelfth and thirteenth centuries, seemingly brought to Europe by returning crusaders.

These short stories, famously called "broader than they are long" by former Harvard Professor Douglas Bush (qtd. in Abrams and Harpham 2014: 122), have generated a great deal of conversation about their intended audiences; first thought to be written for the lower classes, more recent commentary has suggested a noble audience that desired to laugh at a rising bourgeoisie and peasantry.

Charles Muscatine suggests that the fabliaux "show us medieval culture unembarrassedly in the midst of its everyday pleasures and transgressions" (1986: 2). Produced by jongleurs (traveling minstrels) like Gautier le Leu (13th century) and Rutebuf (c. 1245–85), these short poems achieve a kind of unfettered realism about sex, desire, work, and money that is very different from the elevated and detached social world of the romance. Fabliaux often play with gender conventions as well; portraying women as sexually desirous who often came out the victors in the sexual games played upon them, leaving cuckolded husbands in their wake. While a romance might explain adultery through the language of true, elevated love, in the fabliau, adultery is spurned by sexual desire and dissatisfaction, and sometimes just circumstance.

The Old French fabliaux's influence spread in the fourteenth century and appear in their mostly widely known sources, Giovanni Boccaccio's *Decameron* and Chaucer's *Canterbury Tales.* Several fabliaux are found among the 100 tales of the *Decameron*, and the genre seems to be one of Boccaccio's sources, as he draws theme, style, and substance from them to tell his stories. Boccaccio's use of these narratives helps draw critics' attention to their potential; not just ribald stories, the fabliaux themselves often offer morals, and this nexus afforded later poets an opportunity to place the fabliaux against other stories, such as romances, to allow them to comment on each other.

Chaucer also had his fun parodying the romance genre in the Miller's, Reeve's, Cook's, Shipman's, and Merchant's Tales. In each, romance elements such as courtly love and chivalric duty are twisted in some way to form a rowdy and ribald tale with humor as a primary component. Bawdy jokes and nether regions abound in stories such as the Miller's Tale, poking fun at the otherwise stern and serious considerations found in the romance genre. While a knight's quest for love finds fulfillment in a medieval romance, a young lover's desire for the same finds him kissing a bare bottom in a fabliau like the Miller's Tale, in which a love-struck scholar falls in love with a lady who happens to be his old host's young wife. The old carpenter is desperate to keep her away from other men, afraid that he will become a cuckold. Nicholas, however, devises an elaborate plan to not only make the carpenter look like a fool but have his way with Allison as well, completely disregarding the precepts of chivalry and turning courtly love into a game.

And if anyone thinks medieval narrative can't be as erotic as *Fifty Shades of Grey*, think again: in the Merchant's Tale, Damian and May, two young lovers, outsmart jealous old January (much like Nicholas tricks the carpenter John in the Miller's Tale). Walking in the garden with January – a blind, jealous old husband who keeps a hand on her at all times so that he might know her whereabouts – May offers to climb into a tree to pluck a pear. Unbeknownst to him, Damian has already climbed into the tree and waits for the moment May will join him. When she does, under the ruse that she is simply picking fruit for her husband who waits below, Chaucer writes, "I kan not glose, I am a rude man– / And sodeynly anon this Damyan / Gan pullen up the smok, and in he throng" [I cannot gloss over, I am a simple man / And suddenly this Damian / Pulled up her skirt and in he thrust] (Chaucer 1987: CT IV 2151–3 trans. Cunder).

While scenes of intercourse in a medieval romance or fabliau might not be as extensive or detailed as modern romances, they are certainly there for the keen reader. Subtlety has its part to play, both as a result of the time period and the skill of the author, but that does not lessen the emphasis on characters' sexual appetite. As Chaucer clearly demonstrates, the urge to have sex in the Middle Ages was as strong as it is today.

CONCLUSION

For readers of fantasy – whether epic fantasy like *The Lord of the Rings* or the fantasy of modern romance telling the story of a forbidden love – medieval romance combines magic, adventure, and emotion as a way to interrogate and analyze social and cultural values. If today the "romance" genre exclusively refers to a love story, in the Middle Ages, "romance" meant a story that examines the desires and motivations of its characters in all forms. At the same time, those who look askance at formulaic romance novels, and perhaps scoff at their literary validity, will find comrades within the medieval fabliau which perhaps does the same thing in its time – though without invalidating the romance it parodies. For all of its apparent differences from modern-day love stories, the medieval romance remains the genre to which readers should turn if they wish to understand the interiority and emotional struggles found in a courtly and feudal society. And even if contemporary readers don't go out questing for adventure and dragons, they can certainly relate to conflicts of emotion, desire, and duty which still resonate strongly today.

FOR FURTHER READING

PRIMARY TEXTS

Readers interested in the romance might well start with **Chrétien de Troyes (1991).** *Arthurian Romances.* **Trans. William Kibbler and Carleton W. Carroll. London: Penguin**, or *The Lais of Marie de France.* **(1995). Trans. Robert Hanning and Joan Ferrante. Grand Rapids, MI: Baker Books**, as these two authors are often credited with originating the form – or at least articulating an existing tradition. Arthuriana fans might find themselves engaged by *The Lancelot-Grail Reader: Selections from the Medieval French Arthurian Cycle* **(2000). Ed. Norris J. Lacy. New York: Garland**, and might well enjoy **Gottfried von Strassburg's** *Tristan.* **(2004). Trans. Arthur Hatto. London: Penguin**. An intriguing and sometimes troubling romance which focuses on gender is *Silence: A Thirteenth-Century Romance* **(1999). Ed. and Trans. Sarah Roche-Mahdi. East Lansing, MI: Michigan State University Press**. Looking outside the European tradition, readers will find **Nizami. (1997).** *The Story of Layla and Majnun.* **Trans. Rodolf Gelpke. New Lebanon, NY: Omega Publications** a valuable addition.

For those who prefer the lyric side of things, *Lyrics of the Troubadours and Troveres.* **(1973). Ed. and Trans. Frederick Goldin. New York: Anchor** provides an ample selection in facing-page translations, as does *The Women Troubadours.* **(1980). Ed. and Trans. Meg Bogin. New York: W. W. Norton**, which offers a window into the world of the Trobairiz. Anyone looking for humor and parody will enjoy *The Fabliaux.* **(2013). Trans. Nathaniel E. Dubin. New York. W. W. Norton/ Liveright**. There are many anthologies of medieval romances, Breton lais, and lyrics available as well.

SECONDARY SOURCES

There is a great deal of work written about the medieval literature of love, taking a wide range of approaches to the material. Some classic works on romance include **Eugene Vinaver's** *The Rise of Romance* **(1971). Oxford: Oxford University Press** and **Robert W. Hanning's** *The Individual in Twelfth-Century Romance* **(1977). New Haven, CT: Yale University Press**. The former distinguishes romance through its evolution and emergence in the twelfth century, while the latter considers romance to be the first real genre of interiority and individuality. A comprehensive overview is provided by the *Cambridge Companion to Medieval Romance* **(2000). Ed. Roberta L. Kreuger. Cambridge: Cambridge University Press**, which includes articles by notable scholars on all aspects of the genre. **Corrine Sanders's (1993)** *The Forest of Medieval Romance.* **Cambridge: D. S. Brewer** focuses on one of the major landscapes of romance that offers a liminal, and therefore transformative, experience of space. *Pulp Fictions of Medieval England: Essays in Popular Romance* **(2004). Ed. Nicola McDonald. Manchester: Manchester University Press** provides a view into some less-well-known and often bizarre (and problematic) Middle English romances. In addition, there are many volumes on the romances of particular countries, centuries, and authors, as well as many volumes on medieval love and desire. Two particularly interesting works that touch on opposing variations of that subject are **Richard E. Ziekowitz's** *Homoeroticism and Chivalry: Discourses of Male Same-Sex Desire in the Fourteenth Century* **(2003). New York: Palgrave Macmillan** and **Louise M. Sylvester's** *Medieval Romance and the Construction of Heterosexuality* **(2008). New York: Palgrave MacMillan.** *Islamicate Sexualities: Translations across Temporal Geographies of Desire* **(2008). Ed. Kathryn Babayan and Afsaneh Najmabadi. Cambridge, MA: Harvard University Press** considers gender, sexuality, and desire outside of medieval Europe. For readers who wish to explore this subject more broadly, **Tison Pugh's** *Queering Medieval Genres* **(2004). New York: Palgrave Macmillan** examines sexual variation across all the genres discussed in this chapter.

On the lyric, **Sarah Spence's** *Rhetorics of Reason and Desire: Vergil, Augustine, and the Troubadours* **(1988). Ithaca, NY:**

Cornell University Press and *The Voice of the Trobairiz: Perspectives on Women Troubadours* (1989). Ed. **William D. Paden. Philadelphia: University of Pennsylvania Press** provide insight into the largest body of medieval love poetry, while **Peter Dronke's** *The Medieval Lyric* (2002). **Cambridge: Boydell and Brewer** offers an overview beyond medieval Provençe. Fabliau readers will find **Charles Muscatine's** *The Old French Fabliaux* (1986). **New Haven, CT: Yale University Press** a useful introduction; that, and **R. Howard Bloch's** *The Scandal of the Fabliaux* (1986). **Chicago: University of Chicago Press** will provide substantial background to the Middle Ages' most scurrilous genre.

TOUCHING HEAVEN
THE LITERATURE OF RELIGION

The European Middle Ages is always considered the Age of Faith, where peasants and nobles alike believed in their God and the tenets of the Church without much question. Too often this creates a very narrow, static image of the medieval period despite the fact that religious devotion informs a great deal of literature written during the time. However, this material is not unitary in form or content. Even readers of theology will find variations in the approach to and understanding of Church doctrine. Theological works form the largest body of literature from the European Middle Ages, at least in part because the Church was the center of learning and, perhaps more importantly, literacy for a great deal of the period. Important theological discussions in Judaism and Islam are also written during this time, although neither religion has a monastic system that centralizes literary production in the same way. However, doctrinal works, and even philosophical examinations of theological principles, are not the primary concern of this volume. In a larger sense, they are certainly literature, but our focus here is on works engaging more individual experience that reached a wider, more popular audience.

The religious literature of the Middle Ages varies in genre, approach, and purpose, ranging from spiritual autobiography to religious drama, mystical visions to devotional lyrics and sermons. Many hymns were written, some of which are still sung today. One of the most interesting elements of medieval religious literature is its ability to give voice to those whose experiences are not part of the larger doctrinal or theological reach of religious institutions and theological exploration – mystics (male and female), saints, pilgrims, and even some heretics. As with the romance and epic, medieval religious genres often walked the border between the realist and the wildly imaginary; what might be said to differentiate the religious from the secular fantastic is its connection to the divine. A saint or mystic may behave in ways that defy the laws of reality even more than a romance magician, and yet those behaviors are often seen to stem from the saint or mystic's devotion and can even be given directly by God. Medieval religious writing can often stray into worlds that seem very remote and bizarre to a contemporary reader, while at the same time expressing entirely orthodox views. In a sense, they show popular experiences of the theology written by the Church Fathers, but they also show that religion is accessible to all who seek it. These writings can be fictional and fantastic, but they can also be deeply serious and affective in their moral and religious contemplations.

AUGUSTINE'S *CONFESSIONS* AND SPIRITUAL AUTOBIOGRAPHY

Saint Augustine's iconic *Confessions* (397–401 CE) perhaps epitomizes the conversion narrative and sets the stage for future authors who model their work on the internal struggle and spiritual apex Augustine describes in his text. Frederick Van Fleteren describes Augustine as "a bridge between the thought of Ancient Greece, interpreted in the light of the Judeo-Christian Scriptures, and the Middle Ages" (Fleteren 1992: 57), noting Augustine's interweaving of philosophy in the vein of Plotinus and Porphyry (Greek Neo-platonist orators) with religious conversion, and claims that, while "*Confessiones* gives precise details of the author's life… it is much more than an autobiography… [It] uses the author's life to illustrate a universal theory of humanity" (Fleteren 1992: 63). It "can be read as a literary masterpiece, as a work of profound psychological insight, as a philosophical treatise, and as a work of theological genius" (Fleteren 1992: 63), and has survived as a canonical work for over 1600 years.

Perhaps one reason why Augustine's *Confessions* were – and are – so popular is that the book is exactly what its title proclaims: a confession of what the author saw as his own faults and failures, from lasciviousness (which produced an illegitimate son) to pride, along with the conflict between two wills that coexisted within him and a struggle to negotiate the plausible and alluring heretical sects circulating during Augustine's time. The autobiography shows the author as human, as one who plods through life battling the same desires and weaknesses that plague all humankind. One of the prolific quotations from the text – popular even to this day – is Augustine's plea, "*da mihi castitatem et continentam, sed noli modo*" – or "make me chaste and celibate, but not yet" (Augustine *Confessions*, trans. Chadwick 1991: 145). Whether a facetious commentary on an adolescent boy who wants to be holy without giving up earthly pleasures just yet (he says also in Book VIII, "They [his old habits] tugged at the garment of my flesh and whispered: 'Are you getting rid of us?' And 'from this moment we shall never be with you again, not for ever and ever'" [Augustine *Confessions*, trans. Chadwick 1991: 151]) or a deeper investigation of will and predestination (after all, if God determines the path everyone takes through life, how much agency does Augustine [or anyone] really have when it comes to conversion?), the recurrent prayer brings Augustine's humanity to the forefront and allows readers to recognize in him a struggle that likely ran through the veins of many a medieval (and even modern) Christian. Henry Chadwick notes in his introduction to the text that the "contemporary reader today may find much of it so 'modern' that at times it is a shock to discover how very ancient are the presuppositions and the particular context in which the author wrote" (Chadwick 1991: ix).

Later medieval texts often lose this grounding, painting archetypal characters who convert to Christianity after some miraculous event while glossing over the tumultuous reality that converts would often endure while attempting to balance classic philosophies – such as Neoplatonism, which conflicted with various Christian doctrines – against emerging religious thought. Whenever Augustine came up against such a conflict, he would side decisively with Christianity, as Fleteren asserts (1992: 60); but that isn't to say he didn't struggle with reconciling his mode of understanding the world with his commitment to Christian authority – rather, throughout the text, Augustine delicately and profoundly "capture[s] the human search and struggle for happiness and rest" (Fleteren 1992: 64) amid a world of contradictions and incompatibilities.

Fictional conversion accounts such as those told by Chaucer – while brilliant in their own mode and written with a different purpose and to a different audience – often focus on instantaneous conversions rather than any personal conflict or struggle. Conversions happen spontaneously rather than engaging the path along which many converts (Augustine especially) travel(ed). Dan Crawford claims, "To the extent that the conversion process, considered *as a whole*, is a product of [Augustine's] effort and choosing, it *is* his accomplishment" (Crawford 1988: 301, original emphasis). In later fictional texts, the conversions of Saracens, pagans, and nonbelievers serve a different purpose – the expansion of the Christian corpora rather than individual experience – while works such as Dante's *Divine Comedy*, which show powerful Augustinian influence, apply a similar depth of thought and emotional stake inherent in Augustine's transfiguration to the journey of the already-Christian soul to God.

Another central concern with which Augustine grapples in *Confessions* is the concept of the will. Crawford again examines what Augustine describes as an "old will that wills earthly pleasures, and also a 'new will which had come to life in [Augustine]... [but] was not yet strong enough to overcome the old'" (Crawford 1988: 298). Augustine penned another text a few years before *Confessions* titled *De Libero Arbitrio* [On the Free Choice of the Will] (388–395 CE) in which he considers how God, the creator of the will, is not also the creator of sin and evil.

Overall, Augustine's contribution to the literary world marks him as a religious scholar deeply concerned with the trials and nature of humanity. Fleteren notes, regarding the timeless applicability of Augustine's numerous works, that:

> in the High Middle Ages, when the relations between Church and state were being worked out, it was the Augustine of *De Civitate Dei* (The City of God) that was influential. During the Reformation and post-reformation, the works of the Pelagian period on grace as well as the teaching of Christ as the interior master became paramount. During the Renaissance... it was the Augustine of the *De Doctrina Christiana*... Today it is the Augustine of the *Confessions* who reigns.
>
> (Fleteren 1992: 66)

In every age since Augustine lived, his writings have found resonance, whether in university curricula or for the foundation of
religious doctrine. His approach to humanity and to God continues
to offer even modern readers a way to relate to a man who lived so
many centuries ago.

RELIGIOUS RULES AND SERMONS

In addition to religious biographers and autobiographers, writers
such as St. Benedict of Nursia (c. 480 – c. 553 CE) developed
monastic rules for how monks in his order should live their lives
in service to God. The *Rule of St. Benedict* was likely composed in
530 CE, though the precise date is unknown. Scholars have also
debated whether it was written gradually over a period of time or
recorded all at once; regardless, its prologue and seventy-three
chapters – centered around precepts such as poverty, chastity,
obedience, piety, and labor – "constituted by the time of Charlemagne the well-established practice of Western monks, and
later became the basis of new orders like those at Cluny and
Citeaux" (Contemporary Civilization Staff of Columbia College
1960: 175).

While much of the *Rule* may appear dry to the modern reader
uninterested in how medieval monks were to go about their daily
business, there are nonetheless moments of subtle humor
throughout the text such as a detailed paragraph outlining how
monks should sleep. "They shall sleep separately in separate beds,"
Benedict writes, and:

> A candle shall always be burning in that same cell until early in the
> morning. They shall sleep clothed, and girt with belts or with ropes;
> and they shall not have their knives at their sides while they sleep, *lest
> perchance in a dream they should wound the sleepers*... And when they
> rise for the service of God, they shall exhort each other mutually with
> moderation, *on account of the excuses that those who are sleepy are
> inclined to make*.
>
> (Benedict 1960: 180–1, emphasis added)

Again, concerning "whether a monk should be allowed to receive
letters or anything," Benedict orders:

> By no means shall it be allowed to a monk... to receive or to give, without order of the abbot, letters, presents, or any gift, however small... But if [the abbot] order it to be received, it shall be in the power of the abbot to give it to whomever he may will. And the brother to whom it happened to have been sent *shall not be chagrined*; that an opportunity be not given to the devil.
>
> (Benedict 1960: 184, emphasis added)

Though likely intended to be received with all seriousness, this cannot help but be read with a raised eyebrow. How Benedict can presume to order the inward emotions of those under his Rule is perhaps more a medieval mode of thinking than a modern one, and the very inclusion of such a warning indicates that it would not be uncommon for a monk – indeed for anyone – to be at least a little perturbed if a gift sent to him by his family were to be taken and given to someone else.

And yet, those who chose the monastic life in the Middle Ages were prepared to give up such earthly things and focus their lives entirely on service to God, for:

> when any new comer applies for conversion [i.e. to join the Benedictine Order], an easy entrance shall not be granted him... Therefore if he who comes perseveres in knocking, and is seen after four or five days to patiently endure the insults inflicted upon him, and the difficulty of ingress, and to persist in his demand: entrance shall be allowed him, and he shall remain for a few days in the cell of the guests.
>
> (Benedict 1960: 184)

Benedict goes on to list the trials an initiate shall endure, one of which being the proclamation of the *Rule* to him with an admonishment to either accept the *Rule* in its entirety or depart freely. If he accepts, he shall be led to the cell of the novices, and after a lapse of six months, the *Rule* will again be read to him. If he accepts, another four months will test his patience, at which point it will be read a third time. Upon acceptance, he shall be received into the congregation and shall not be allowed to depart from there nor "shake free his neck from the yoke of the Rule" (Benedict 1960: 184–5).

More straightforward is the invocation to poverty by which all monks in the order abide. Benedict proclaims that the monks "should have absolutely not anything: neither a book, nor tablets nor a pen – nothing at all" (Benedict 1960: 181) and that "all things shall be common to all, as it is written: 'Let not any man presume or call anything his own'" (Benedict 1960: 181). Benedict clarifies "whether all ought to receive necessaries equally" and qualifies that there should be "a consideration for infirmities," though "he who needs more, let him be humiliated on account of his infirmity" (Benedict 1960: 181–2).

The *Rule*, then, is an elaborate system that regulates every aspect of a monk's life as part of the Benedictine Order. It sets out directions for eating (how much and when); prayer; manual labor; earthly possessions; sleeping (how and where, including provisions that all should sleep together unless the space be too small; then they should sleep by tens or twenties); and for how to behave with humility and obedience. It is a practical manifesto rather than a mystical vision or autobiographical conversion narrative, seeking to establish order during a time when monasteries and abbeys were spreading rapidly throughout the West and had little guidance on how best to regulate their members, whose monastic life was "looked upon as the ideal existence by the philosophers of the Middle Ages" (Columbia 1960: 175).

Despite the apparently stringent *Rule* of the Benedictines, there were still those in the Middle Ages such as Saint Bernard of Clairvaux who "was a severe critic of the Benedictine order, which he regarded as lax and undisciplined" (Hala 1999: 27). Certainly, if he believed the *Rule* to be lax, his own beliefs on discipline understandably "estranged his followers" at times (Hala 1999: 27). His own life is the subject of a hagiography written by his contemporaries titled *Vita prima Bernardi* (later translated in the twentieth century by Geoffrey Webb and Adrian Walker), and he is known for both his loyal devotion to friends and his vehement attacks on his enemies, focusing his angst in one particular letter against the Benedictines of Cluny who, he claims, influenced his young nephew – really his cousin – Robert to defect from the Cistercians of Clairvaux where Bernard served as abbot. "A credulous innocent was led astray so that a soul for whom Christ died was lost to Cluny," Hala paraphrases Bernard's response, noting further

Bernard's incitement that "a terrible judgment awaits Cluny for its misdeeds and laxity" (Hala 1999: 29).

This venomous anger comes from the same man who preached the centrality of love in his sermons – and yet who also advocated for the Second Crusade. Bernard's first known formal treatise, *De gradibus humilitatis et superbiae* [The Steps of Humility and Pride], written in 1124 or 1125, is considered to be an expansion and elaboration of the seventh chapter of St. Benedict's *Rule* in which the twelve steps of humility are outlined. In it, Bernard demonstrates his affinity for metaphor and rhetorical device, framing his contemplative, mystic, and affective theology. Throughout his sermons, he focuses on explaining his theological beliefs, along with a display of "distinctive traits: [he] scrupulously matches his form and style to his content; human experience is almost always the starting point for even his loftiest visions; and he seems to know the minds of his readers, using that knowledge to manipulate them" (Hala 1999: 36). Bernard died on 20 August 1153, leaving his task of revising and editing his entire collection of works unfinished. In 1174, Bernard was canonized as a saint before being declared a doctor of the Church in 1830, impressing upon his contemporaries and his successors the image of a man who violently defended his beliefs and fought tirelessly to promote the way of life he felt would best bring people to God.

Benedict's *Rule* was the founding example for monastic houses, but many other guides to religious life existed in the Middle Ages. Guides for Anchoresses – women who chose to be isolated in small spaces (some in small anchorholds within churches, others outside the community) to live a fulfilled religious life – provided instruction on how to turn their desires towards God and how to exile themselves from the world both literally and figuratively. The thirteenth-century *Ancrene Wisse* or *Ancrene Riwle* [Way or Rule for Anchoresses], written for three women seeking to enter the contemplative life, consists of eight chapters; one and eight deal with the "Outer Rule," or the anchoresses' exterior life – these provide bookends around the middle chapters focusing on the more important "Inner Rule," or interior life. More allegorical than Benedict's practical approach, the *Ancrene Wisse* compares the anchoresses to various sorts of birds with allegorical features as a method of regulating the inner life, and offers antidotes to the temptations of the seven deadly sins. The physical senses must be turned into spiritual, interior senses, so that only good comes through them, rather than experience of the outside world. God's love, the text suggests, is like Greek Fire, a medieval poison gas, able to destroy all enemies in its path, and the love of God, which the text describes in highly courtly and somewhat erotic terms, is a greater devotion than any suffering or pain brought on by penance. *Hali Meðod* [Holy Method], an instructive sermon written c. 1182–98, offers anchoresses a guide to virginity and the value of spiritual marriage to God over secular, earthly marriage. This opening text of the Katherine Group of poems is accompanied by works praising the virginity of Saints Juliana of Nicomedia, Margaret of Antioch, and Catherine of Alexandria, who provide the anchoresses with both inspiration and models of ideal behavior.

Rules for religious life provide a great deal more than formulae for religious practice; charting what is regulated offers a pattern of actual behavior, a sense of what life may have been like for medieval subjects who chose varying kinds of religious life, as well as how the medieval world viewed both body and soul, the material and the spiritual world, and perhaps most importantly, their intersection.

SAINTS' LIVES, MIRACLES OF THE VIRGIN, AND HAGIOGRAPHY

The Lives of the Saints – first the early Christian martyrs, but increasingly monastic and historical saints as the Middle Ages went on – provided a popular source of literary entertainment and instruction. These biographies provided access to history, inspiration, and legend in their recordings of lives, deeds, martyrdoms, and miracles of the saintly community. Jacobus de Voragine (c. 1230–98) compiled the *Legenda Aurea* [Golden Legend], an iconic hagiographical collection, from multiple sources. This encyclopedic text retained its popularity throughout the medieval period. His legends often began with a meditative etymology on the saint's name, followed by the stories of their lives and the miracles attributed to them and their relics after death. Jacobus' work inspired secular and religious writers throughout the Middle Ages, influencing vernacular hagiographic collections like the poetic *South English*

Legendary (13th–14th century) and authors from Dante to Guillaume de Machaut to Christine de Pizan.

Saints' lives were not restricted to the lives of early Christian martyrs, however; hagiography remained a living tradition and a way to valorize and establish the importance of local saints and religious figures (not all of whom were canonized). Hagiography became an important way to vivify pilgrimage sites, as they told of the miracles attributed to the relics held there, while others sought to cement local history, figures, and traditions.

In the thirteenth century, Jacques de Vitry (c. 1160/70–1240) and his disciple, Thomas de Cantimpré (1201–72) wrote a series of "Lives" of holy Beguines of Liège, particularly Marie of Oignies, whose *Vita* Jacques began and Thomas finished. Paralleling these beguines – female religious lay communities particular to the Low Countries in the thirteenth to sixteenth centuries – to priests in power, despite their functioning outside of the established Church, Jacques and Thomas sought to legitimize the work of these communities and preserve the histories of their exemplary women. Thomas's Lives of Margaret of Ypres, Lutgard of Aywières, and most notoriously St. Christina the Astonishing, tell stories of intense devotional practice, spiritual leadership and guidance, and miracles. The last of these lives, called the *Vita Christina Mirabilis* [the Life of St. Christina the Astonishing] tells the story of Christina, who, resurrected from death and having seen a vision of hell, seemed to suffer purgatorial penance on earth, engaging in strange behaviors like standing in an icy river up to her neck, throwing herself into ovens, tying herself to the mill wheel as it circled in and out of the water, wailing, weeping, and rolling herself into a ball in prayer. All attempts by the locals to stop her were unsuccessful; in prison she fed herself with oil that dripped from her breasts. Only their prayers to God mitigated her behavior, which while somewhat less astonishing, remained peculiar in her pursuit of her and others' salvation. Finally dying after two more resurrections, Christina was put to rest in 1224. Thomas's *Vita,* while preserving a compelling, if problematic, story, also authorizes the context of her behaviors as divine rather than demonic, allowing her future canonization by the Church (she remains the patron saint of the mentally ill); in 1992, rock musician Nick Cave and the Bad Seeds turned her legend into a popular song.

The hagiography provided a model for secular authors as well; while Chaucer's second nun tells the tale of St. Cecilia out of the *South English Legendary*, several of his other tales – the Man of Law's tale of Constance, the Physician's tale of Virginia, the Clerk's Tale of Patient Griselda, and the Prioress's tale of the Little Clergeon – all follow a hagiographic model, even if none of the figures actually achieve sanctification in their stories, at least in part because of their fictionality.

DREAM VISIONS, MYSTICS, AND RELIGIOUS LYRIC

Elizabeth Avilda Petroff, a leading scholar of medieval visionary literature, notes:

> Mysticism has been called "the science of the love of God," and "the life which aims at union with God." Mystics may be found in every religious tradition, sometimes as central participants but often on the periphery of accepted practice, for they map out new experiences of the divine.
>
> (Petroff 1991: 6)

One medieval literary version of mystical experience was the dream vision, a form with both religious and secular examples. This trope had the author falling asleep and dreaming an entire narrative, often (but not always) inspired by earthly experience. The medieval ur-dream-vision was Boethius's *Consolation of Philosophy*, in which Boethius, imprisoned falsely and awaiting execution, is comforted and brought to right thinking by Lady Philosophy who appears to him as he laments his abandonment by Fortune. While not specifically Christian, Boethius's text engages many questions about how to prepare oneself for the death that found expression in medieval examples; Lady Philosophy's discourse leads Boethius to examine the nature of honor, the world, and finally the divine. While Dante's *Divine Comedy* follows the dream vision formula, Dante the poet insists that the vision itself is not a dream, unlike Marie de France's *Saint Patrick's Purgatory* (12th century), a pre-Dantean vision of the afterlife. Other examples include the Old English *Dream of the Rood* (10th century), in which the wooden cross of Christ speaks and tells the story of the crucifixion, and the twelfth-century Latin *De Planctu Naturae* of Alan de Lille, in which the author dreams of Nature explaining its inferiority to God.

One of the best-known religious dream visions is William Langland's *Vision of Piers the Plowman* (c. 1270–90), in which Will (both the author's name and an allegory for humanity) falls into a slumber and has a vision of a "fair field full of folk" between a high tower (heaven) and a deep valley (hell). Will meets figures such as Holy Church, Lady Mede, Conscience, and Reason. In a second dream, Piers the Plowman appears, urging the folk in the field to help him plough it; Piers seeks pardon for the people's sins, especially idleness, and meets Truth. Extensive visions of allegorical figures follow, until Piers is revealed to be Christ, and Will discovers the power of Conscience and Grace in defeating the Antichrist. The three versions, known as the A, B, and C texts, attest to the development and popularity of the story, and the popularity of the form is shown in numerous examples throughout the Middle Ages (although some of the best known, such as Guillaume de Lorris' and Jean de Meun's *Roman de la Rose*; Chaucer's *Book of the Duchess, House of Fame, Parliament of Fowles*, and *Legend of Good Women*; and Christine de Pizan's *Chemin de Long Estude*, are primarily secular visions).

Waking dreams, or religious visions, were also well represented in medieval literature, as mystics detailed their visionary experiences. While what promoted these visions varied as much as the authors who experienced them, they share a sense of deep communion with God which enlightens the mystic about divine meanings in ways both intellectual and visceral. Visions range from ecstatic union between God and the soul to contemplation of scripture and prayers. Mystics were found both inside the Church and among the laity, and mysticism was part of the experience of Church figures known more for intellectual theological examinations such as Augustine, Bernard of Clairvaux, and Thomas Aquinas.

Mystical experience was one area in which religious women – nuns, beguines, and laywomen – found an outlet for expression throughout the Middle Ages, although the method of their textual production and dissemination varied. Visionary experience afforded women access to power within the world, which may account for the great extent of this body of work. While some visionary women were primarily written about (such as some of the earliest mystics like Saint Perpetua and Saint Macrina), increasingly throughout the period others wrote or dictated their experiences directly. Figures like Angela of Foligno (c. 1240–1309), a tertiary anchoress in Italy, and Hildegard of Bingen (1098–1179) recorded their mystical experiences; in the *Scivias* (1151–2), Hildegard experiences visions of the Trinity, Creation, the Church, and the Sacraments, all leading to an understanding of the coming Kingdom of God. Illustrated with thirty-five miniatures, the text provides visual and verbal explanation of her experience. In the introduction, Hildegard says that at age forty-two, she was commanded by God to produce the text and share the visions she had experienced most of her life. Hildegard's expressed humility and anxiety about the project, and her need to consult with Church authorities such as Bernard of Clairvaux attests to her concern about making her private experience public, as well as fear that as a woman, she would be subject to significant criticism. The humility *topos*, a sense that the mystic is merely the vessel and mouthpiece for God's word, begins many of these authors' works.

The aforementioned beguines, who gave rise to saintly figures like Christina Mirabilis and Marie of Oignies, also counted mystics among their numbers. One prominent example is Mechtild of Magdeburg (c. 1207 – c. 1294), who composed the *Das fließende Licht der Gottheit* [*Flowing Light of Divinity (or Godhead)*] between 1250 and 1280. Writing in the vernacular, she was known for showing German to be a fitting language to express divine and holy ideas, and while she passed her visions on to male authorities for authentication, she wrote them down in their originary form herself, rather than using a male scribe as others, such as Hildegard and Margery Kempe, did. Her visions are known for being descriptive and passionate, particularly her images of hell, and she feminizes the soul, referring to it throughout as "she." In her first vision, at the age of twelve, she is greeted by the Holy Ghost, who continued to visit her for the rest of her life, influencing her first to join the beguines at Magdeburg and later a Cistercian convent. These encounters, she says, surge "from the Flowing Godhead by many channels into the arid soul, ever bringing fresh knowledge and holier revelation" (Mechtild, trans. Petroff 1986: 214). Her visions of hell were thought to have influenced Dante, whose figure Matelda, in Purgatory, may be named for her, although clear evidence for this is lacking.

England, too, had strong visionary traditions. Anonymous works like the *Cloud of Unknowing* (c. 1375) offered instruction on mystical and contemplative prayer, while Richard Rolle (c. 1300–49) and Walter Hilton (c. 1340–96) wrote of their particular visions. In the *Incendium Amoris* [Fire of Love], Rolle told of three different kinds of mystical experiences: physical warmth, sweetness, and heavenly music. His visions also revealed a set of stages one needed to pass through to become closer to God, clearly connected to his own experiences: the open door, the heat, song, and sweetness.

Rolle's English contemporary, Julian of Norwich (1342 – c. 1420) penned a collection of texts jointly titled *Revelations of Divine Love*, in which she describes a miraculous vision she experienced in the year 1373 on May 8 during a bout of serious illness. That is perhaps the only concrete fact known about Julian of Norwich – the name "Julian" itself isn't even that of the writer, but rather of a church in the city where she lived, and where she eventually walled herself in, living in a room annexed to Saint Julian's church – in addition to vague information such as her seclusion as an anchorite for the majority of her life, living in a sealed room with limited contact with the outside world, though she never became a nun or officially joined any religious order or organization, remaining a layperson throughout her isolation.

Julian of Norwich did have visitors, though, the most notable of which was Margery Kempe, a contemporary of Julian as well as a fellow mystic and spiritual writer. Kempe recorded her visit to Julian in *The Book of Margery Kempe*, a text similar – and yet so disparate – from Julian's own. Whereas Julian remained secluded and shut out from the world, Kempe traveled England, preaching, weeping, and often seen as "a religious type of Alison of Bath, filled with the vitality and vigor of antipatriarchal dissent" (Armstrong 1994: 213). Julian, on the other hand, focused more on showing God's love to her readers, recording the compassion she felt throughout her vision and commenting on the loving humility of a creator God. In one particular instance, she notes a vision of Christ's bleeding head immediately followed by the depiction of a hazelnut in the palm of her hand. She understands this image as a representation of vulnerability balanced by the overwhelming knowledge that all things exist within three properties: "The first is that God made

[them]. The second is that God loves [them]. The third is that God keeps [them]" (Armstrong 1994: 215).

Julian pushes this concept further with her rendering of Christ as a maternal lover. While depictions of God as mother appear in previous religious writings, Julian's "does not divide God into the stern father and kind mother, as earlier traditions had done" (Armstrong 1994: 215). Chapter 59 of the text introduces a new mantra for understanding the "I Am" of the Hebrew Torah: "I am the goodness of the fatherhood; I am the wisdom of the motherhood. I am the light and the grace that is all blessed love. I am the trinity. I am the unity." This conflation of man and woman into one God brings together the sexes in a unique way, restoring, as Bradley suggests in her book *Julian's Way* (1992), "men and women to full humanity" (Armstrong 1994: 215–6).

Margery Kempe led a somewhat different life than Julian of Norwich, though her autobiography "conforms to various patterns of religious life set forth in the hagiographic, devotional, and mystical writings that were so influential in her day" (Despres 1994: 217). Although illiterate herself, she dictated her life's story to two priests who recorded the narrative in two volumes. In it, she describes her marriage to John Kempe and her subsequent desire to depart from the norms of medieval married life. She and her husband eventually took formal vows of chastity after twenty years of marriage when she began her independent life as a pilgrim around the age of forty. It wasn't until after the age of sixty that Margery began to formally record her life without the benefit of notes, maps, or diaries (Despres 1994: 220). Thus, while it might lack chronological form, it adheres to other medieval spiritual autobiographies, including the aforementioned *Confessions*, employing a "tripartite mystical structure... [and] open[ing] with the experience of sickness and conversion – a common pattern in hagiography and mystical writings" (Despres 1994: 220). It also mimics medieval romance narratives with Kempe's own "quest" or "pilgrimage" and "return," and even follows the pattern of Christ's life with his ministry, suffering, and ultimately his death.

Accompanying these religious visions were a large body of religious lyrics – poems, meditations, and songs to God, the Virgin Mary, Saints, the Cross, and other religious subjects. These often drew elements from courtly love traditions to express the speaker's desire for the divine; Jesus is in places described as lover and husband, while Mary receives the same adulation, in much the same terms, as any courtly lady. The Middle English lyric, "Swete Jesu, King of blisse," begins "Swete Jesu, King of blisse / Min herte love, min herte lisse / Thou are swete mid iwisse" [Sweet Jesus, King of bliss / My heart loves, my heart desires / You are truly sweet] (Luria and Hoffman 1974: 99; translation Angela Jane Weisl). Despite the use of the first person, the lyrics are not particularly personal; rather, the first person narration becomes the voice of any member of the community who sings, speaks, or reads them, allowing them to participate in a shared experience. Early Middle English cycles, such as the thirteenth-century Katherine Group and Wohunge (or Wooing) Group, show the richness of the form, but also their use, as these were guides for anchoresses on how to focus their desires on the Divine, rather than on things of the world. Turning secular language religious, these poems offered an outlet for passionate feelings without the dangers that those could pose to someone who had chosen religious life.

RELIGIOUS DRAMA

Drama, at least until the later Middle Ages, was primarily religious, finding origins in a Church that sought to instruct a largely illiterate population in its teachings by staging biblical events on particular feast and fast days. Very little of the classical dramatic tradition remained after the fall of the Roman Empire in 476 CE, when people's dramatic experience was replaced instead by Church performances of sacraments. The theater was considered a threat to Christianity; various Church Fathers including Augustine viewed it as an instrument of the devil because of its potential to corrupt the soul, while acting was considered a mocking of God's creation. Thus, a new tradition of dramatization of biblical stories and liturgical moments emerged within the Church itself, taking this sinful form and making it an instrument of instruction. Performance could teach both biblical history and theology, as well as providing a method by which the congregation could experience the affective content of the holiday emotionally.

The earliest liturgical drama is often considered to be the *Quem Quaeritis* ["Whom do you seek?"] performance at Easter c. 925, in which two choirs situated in different places in the church sang back and forth to each other the words exchanged between the Angel and the three Marys at Christ's tomb, three days after the crucifixion. The *Regularis* Concordia, written c. 965 CE by Æthelwold of Winchester, contains stage directions and a script for this trope, showing how quickly it caught on as a method of liturgical performance.

One of Europe's first dramatists was Hrotsvit of Gandersheim (c. 935–973), a canoness in the Abbey of Gandersheim. She was presumably of noble parentage given the status of the Abbey, which had been granted complete freedom from secular rule by Otto I, about whom Hrotsvit wrote an adulatory poem. Under the noble Abbess Geberga (c. 940–1001), Gandersheim Abbey was a center for cultural, literary, and religious life, and it was in this atmosphere that Hrotsvit composed her plays and poems. The dramas, all on religious subjects, were responses to the Roman dramatist Terence, so Hrotsvit may be said to have been one of the medieval religious authors who preserved remnants of the classical tradition for a Christian audience. As Katherina Wilson notes in her collection of Hrotsvit's works, "she considers hermitic life (total solitude in worship) and martyrdom as the two most privileged manifestations of Christian devotion" (1998: 3), and her plays offer both as solutions to the sins of the world. While some, such as "Sapientia" and "Dulcitius" tell the stories of young virgins who challenge great Kings in order to continue to pursue their Christian faith, ultimately converting many before achieving ascension through glorious martyrdom, "Pafnutius" and "Abraham" focus instead on women who have strayed into prostitution and are brought back into the fold of the faithful by learned men who convince them of their wrongs, put them in anchorholds to contemplate their sins, and ultimately release them so they can ascend, renewed, into heaven. Other plays take on other salutary themes such as conversion and moral desire; "Callimacus" shows postulants choosing death over dishonor, which ultimately leads to rebirth – first on earth and then in heaven.

Despite their often masculine titles, the plays focus on female spirituality and potential – perhaps unsurprising given Hrotsvit's own situation and interests – showing female potential to spread the faith, while simultaneously advocating for the virtues of virginity and chastity. However, in Hrotsvit's dramas, no one willing to accept and repent his or her sins is truly fallen; the harlots Mary and Thaïs are able to achieve salvation through reclaimed belief and intense penance, and the seducer Callimachus is redeemed by metaphorically following the same path as Drusiana; she literally dies to escape his advances so that she might live in heaven, and his experiences in her tomb lead him to grace. However, Fortunatus, who led Callimachus to Drusiana's body so that he might violate it in death, chooses literal death and damnation in the sight of Drusiana's resurrection and Callimachus's conversion. In this case, and in "Gallicianus," and the two martyrdom plays, women are agents of conversion, able, through their moral action and corporeal incorruptibility, to lead many to the faith.

There is much discussion and no satisfactory resolution on either side about whether Hrotsvit's plays were ever performed. Some contain highly dramatic scenes, such as Dulcitius embracing pots and pans, thinking he is violating the young virgins in prison, or Drusiana's resurrection; indeed, they also all contain a great deal of complex symbolism, use of musical and mathematic parallels to elucidate themes of chaos and harmony, examinations of the nature of good and evil, and investigations of Christian virtues. Clearly educated in the classics and the philosophy and theology of her day, Hrotsvit, "like St. Augustine, presents the problem of evil within the context of opposites" (Wilson 1985: 11). Wilson notes, of Hrotsvit's works, "her texts seek adherence to the monastic ideal and to an epistemology which confirms that truth, that is revealed truth, is recognizable, absolute, eternal and imitable; a truth persuasively conveyed for the moral edification of her readers" (Wilson 1998: 15).

Liturgical drama spread widely throughout Europe in the twelfth and thirteenth centuries, with evidence from places as disparate as Russia, Scandinavia, and Italy. Plays such as the *Jeu de Saint Nicholas* [Mystery of St. Nicholas] (c. 1200) by Jean Bodel and the *Jeu d'Adam* [Mystery of Adam] (c. 1150) offered edification and entertainment. The latter offers stage directions, suggesting that it was performed outside, making it a transition to one of the largest bodies of religious drama, the cycle plays. These plays told the entire cycle of Christian history from the creation to the apocalypse; unlike previous examples, they were performed not by the

Church, but by laymen in public settings, reaching an increasingly larger audience.

In the High Middle Ages, trade guilds took on the performance of plays, generally biblically based. The plays were often associated in some way with their particular trade; for instance, bakers often performed the play of the Last Supper, while goldsmiths often took on the play of the nativity because of their ability to produce an effective star. Performed in pageant wagons resembling modern-day trailer stages, plays became one of the leading examples of public literary experience. Their mobility allowed for changes of venue, both for dramatic purposes and to provide access to the widest possible range of audiences. These cycles, called the Mystery Plays in the British Isles, were widely performed and are preserved in four cycles: York (forty-eight plays), the *Ludus Coventriae* [sometimes called Coventry] (forty-two), Wakefield (thirty-two), and Chester (twenty-four). Many additional plays, such as the Norwich Grocers' Play or the Brome *Abraham and Isaac*, survive without the rest of their cycles.

These plays had a primarily educational and didactic function; they did not often have the same symbolic content as Hrotsvit's dramas, for instance, although they shared their moral and salutary focus. That said, they were not without their dramatic moments, such as the mock nativity in the Wakefield *Second Shepherd's Play*, or the fight between Noah and his Wife in the Wakefield *Noah*. The Brome *Abraham and Isaac* play, with its staged moment of near sacrifice, and the plays of the crucifixion that it paralleled, doubtless incited profound emotions of pathos and terror in their viewers. Clearly, too, the plays' authors and performers saw the value of comedy, generally played out by devils and demons, which both entertained audiences and showed how insignificant the powers of Satan were in the face of those of the Divine.

While the British mystery cycles are the largest body of surviving dramas from this period, many dramas from the continent also survive; indeed, evidence of religious drama exists in nearly every country in Europe. Actors were no longer clergy, but members of the populace, who were engaged in every aspect of the performance.

Along with the cycle dramas, this period saw the performance of morality plays, which provided lessons for laymen about how to lead their lives with the goal of heaven. Like Hrotsvit's dramas, they suggested that any sinner capable of sincere repentance could achieve salvation, no matter how deep the sin. *Everyman*, perhaps the best known of this genre, tells the story of Everyman who, hearing Death's call, searches for someone to accompany him to his last judgment. Rejected by Kindred, Cousin, and Goods (symbolizing his earthly possessions), he discovers that only his Good Deeds will go with him to the grave, weak and neglected as they have been; his sincere understanding of his failures leads to a salvific conclusion. In a similar vein are *Mankinde* and the *Castle of Perseverance*, the latter of which depicts mankind's journey from birth to death, a microcosm of the larger cycle dramas. However different medieval drama may be from contemporary theater, in its long history and its didactic power, it is a rich achievement.

QUEST FOR THE HOLY GRAIL ROMANCES

Religious material even found itself the subject of more secular genres. Now considered an essential trope of the Middle Ages and the Arthurian narrative, popular in medieval films from *Excalibur* to *Monty Python and the Holy Grail*, the Quest for the Holy Grail appears first c. 1190 in Chrétien de Troyes' unfinished romance, *Perceval, or the Conte de Graal*. The Grail – a cup or dish with mystical powers – is not described as holy. The origin of the Grail myth may be Celtic, as there are many magic cauldrons and vessels in the Celtic tradition, which has its own connection to the courtly romance through the Breton *lai*; however, no surviving texts make this explicit. Chrétien's story attracted many redactors, interpreters, and continuators, each with their own interpretation of the Grail in the twelfth and thirteenth centuries. Wolfram van Essenbach, one of the best known, imagined the Grail as a sort of meteorite that fell from the sky, albeit a holy one. Wulfram combines Chrétien's story with Robert de Boron's late-twelfth-century *Joseph d'Arimathie*, from which the association of the Grail with Jesus seems to stem. Boron identifies the Grail as the vessel from the Last Supper which Joseph used at the crucifixion to catch Christ's blood. Joseph is thrown into prison, where he is visited and instructed by Christ; once released, he heads west towards Europe and founds a dynasty of Grail Keepers. This led the Grail legend and the Holy Chalice to be interwoven, connecting the mysticism of Chrétien's symbolic object with the mysteries of the Eucharist, and the Grail emerges as a specifically Christian symbol in later versions of the Percival story in the Vulgate Cycle, the Post-Vulgate Cycle, and Thomas Malory's *Morte Darthur*.

In Chrétien's romance, Perceval visits the home of the Fisher King and witnesses a spectacular procession of objects including a bleeding lance, candelabra, and finally a (notably, Chrétien does not call it *the*) Grail. Because the dish carried only a wafer – the Fisher King's meal – and the association with the bleeding lance, a Christian connection may be implied. In addition, Perceval's failure to ask about what he sees prevents his healing of the Fisher King's wound, which certainly has metaphoric similarities to the duty of the Christian to heal the world and bring on the second coming. In any case, it is easy to see how Chrétien's Grail can metamorphose into a holy object.

The Christian Holy Grail quests are best exemplified in the *Quest de Saint Graal* [Quest for the Holy Grail] (c. 1210), part of the larger *Lancelot-Grail* or Vulgate cycle of Arthurian romances. Fusing the Arthurian story with Christian symbolism throughout, the Grail serves as a centerpiece to determine the true value of the Christian knight. In it, a new Grail hero emerges; while Perceval remains a key figure, the saintly Galahad, son of Lancelot and the daughter of the Fisher King, descended from King David and the family of Grail Keepers, emerges as the only one worthy of seeing the Grail and understanding its mysteries. All the knights – Lancelot, Gawain, Bors, Perceval, and Galahad – are tested on their journeys in physical and mystical ways, and each is judged according to his deeds and his behaviors. The *Quest* blends secular romance, tragedy, and mysticism, making it distinct from Chrétien's *Perceval* and its continuations, even those that interpret the Grail through a Christian lens. In the *Quest* and the Grail-romances that follow, the desired object of the quest becomes a kind of religious ineffability, nearly unattainable, a symbol of mankind's complex and challenged search for divine grace. As such, it offers a challenge to the courtly romance and the world that produces it. As Pauline Matarasso says in her introduction to the Penguin translation of the poem:

> The *Quest* sets out to reveal the inadequacies and the dangers of the courtly ideal. By allowing his heroes to retain their traditional roles

and character, the author is able to show how their much-vaunted
attributes lead them to the outcome one would least have looked for;
the last are perhaps not first, but he makes no bones about showing
how the first are last.

(Matarasso 2005: 15)

The poem, Matarasso notes, shows that the secrets of the Holy
Grail are the mysteries of the Eucharist revealed; grace is freely
given to all, but individuals only receive it to the extent that they are
capable. Only the completely pure of heart and body, like Galahad,
can attain the fully ecstatic union with the divine, to "contemplate
in love what 'the heart of man cannot conceive nor the tongue
relate'" (2005: 16). The knights in the poem demonstrate various
levels of spiritual development; if Galahad is a human-saint, Perceval
is childlike in his simplicity, which lets him abandon himself to
God but also to some very unwise decisions and near despair; Bors,
well-meaning and prudent, and instructed in divine teachings,
makes only reasoned choices, but is never open to full feeling as a
result. Lancelot and Gawain show how paragons of Knighthood
may not be perfect Christians; Lancelot cannot escape the burden
of his past sins, and Gawain, despite his good intentions and
eagerness to go on the quest, cannot escape his knightly values to
espouse his Christian ones; his drive for prowess and *avanture*
ultimately lead to destructive bloodshed, made horrifying as he
discovers he is slaughtering not enemies but his fellow knights of
the round table. Thus, the *Quest of the Holy Grail* and its medieval
descendants becomes a romance that undermines the values of
romance and a poem that suggests the greatest spiritual value is in
the ineffable; it is a text that finally undoes itself in complex ways.

Many contemporary theories about the Grail exist; for a time,
the Antioch Chalice, currently held at the Metropolitan Museum
of Art, was thought to be the Holy Grail, because it is the first
Christian artifact to depict Christ and his disciples on the exterior
casing which sheaths an inner, older cup. Novels like Dan Brown's
DaVinci Code (2003) have played on an association of the Holy
Grail with the Knight's Templar. These may be more successful at
holding contemporary interest than the *Quest de Saint Graal*, yet
both retain a preoccupation with the potential of a symbolic object
that embodies a sacred history.

OVIDE MORALISÉ

One of the most popular books of the Middle Ages, if a text's number of surviving manuscripts is an accurate measure, was the *Ovide Moralisé*, or moralized Ovid, one of the most culturally and literarily important texts you've never heard of. Although there are many versions of the work, a version of Ovid's *Metamorphoses* (with reference to other Ovidian works and additional classical and medieval sources), in both vernacular and Latin, the "essential" *Ovide Moralisé* is the version written in French at the same time as Dante wrote the *Divine Comedy* and edited by an anonymous Franciscan author. It was one of the major sources of information about the pagan gods and classical mythology, "moralized" to fit into a Christian universe with the addition of approximately 60,000 lines of commentary, philosophical and theological, to Ovid's text, making most exegesis longer than the stories on which it comments. In this vein, it followed earlier commentators, such as Fulgentius (c. 5th-6th century CE) and Bernardus Silvestris (c. 1140), who read the *Aenied* in a detailed moral, philosophical, and Christian context. The commentary – informed by the Bible, authorities both religious and secular, classical and medieval – was composed as a way to incorporate the Ovidian tradition into a Christian world. In it, every character, symbol, and narrative is employed to put forward a didactic meaning. Reading and understanding Ovid, its author suggests, leads to a Beatific Vision of Paradise, achievable if readers overcome the earthly desires and misplaced affections that drive Ovid's characters. Miranda Griffin aptly describes the project:

> fusing references to and tales from diverse medieval and classical sources, the *Ovide moralisé* is a microcosm of the late medieval library, offering a digest of myth and doctrine, and manifesting a reading practice aware of its reliance on, and reassessment of, previous instances of authority.
>
> (Griffin 2015: 201)

NON-CHRISTIAN RELIGIOUS WORKS

The medieval religious world was not exclusively Christian. While an obvious statement, it is often occluded by the articulation of a

Western medieval tradition presented as united by the Roman Church and uniform in its religious expression. An examination of the works discussed above will show that within orthodox Christianity, there remained a wide range of opportunities for expression, experience, and devotion. And indeed, writings from heretical sects like the Albigensians earlier in the period, and Lollards in England in the fourteenth century, show that while the Church may have exerted political domination, other varieties of essentially Christian religious experience and thought were still taking place. However, to get a full view of the religious literature of the Middle Ages, it is vital to expand one's reading and thinking beyond Christian Europe.

In the twelfth century, at the same time that the Christian mystical tradition was developing in Europe, Sufism, or Islamic Mysticism, was rising in Egypt, and it continued to spread in area and popularity into the fourteenth century. Religious philosophers such as Ibn-Sina (980–1037), known as Avicena in the West, and Ibn-Rushd (1126–98), known as Averroes, were applying Aristotelian principles to Islamic theology and writing on metaphysics, logic, and medicine. Both were interested in rationalism in the face of Islamic mystical traditions, particularly that of Al Ghazali (1058–1111). Persian Sufi poet Jalaladdin Rumi's (1207–73) *Maṭnawīye Ma'nawī* (Spiritual Couplets), a six-volume work of his verses, bound together scenes from everyday life, Quranic exegesis, prophesy, song, and stories into a complex tapestry that was both deeply connected to the details of his Islamic faith and unifying in its outlook, suggesting that the divine presence does not forget people of other religions. In his poetry and his prose works – mostly collections of his teachings by his students – he advocated for a deep mystical spirituality that led the soul to the love of the divine. However, for Rumi, this journey was not an end in itself; the soul – purged of ego and enlightened by its experience – then returned to the world to inspire others. He advocated singing and dancing as pathways for the soul to reach God, and his poetry continues to be interpreted musically today. His contemporary popularity reaches across religious traditions and languages, and he was recently cited as being the most popular poet in the United States (Ciabattari 2014).

Judaism enjoyed a significant lyric tradition, with a large body of *piyuut*, or religious poems, written from the seventh to the eighth

centuries, particularly in the Holy Land. Yehuda Halevi (c. 1075–
1141) and Simon Ben Yehudah ibn Gabriol (11th century), in
Spain, applied Arabic poetic forms to Hebrew religious (and secular)
poetry. Halevi, originally interested in rational philosophy, shifted
to a belief in faith and revelation, and felt that a true knowledge of
God could only come in the land of Israel, where God's presence
was strongest. He outlined his ideas in the *Kuzari*, although many of
them are articulated more viscerally in his poetry. At the end of his
life, he took a journey to Israel where he died. Poems leading up to
the journey meditated extensively on pilgrimage and travel.

Jewish medieval literature also includes the *kabbalistic* mystical
tradition. *Kabbalah* seeks to uncover the divine structure of all
being, and sees the Torah and even its letters as synonymous with
God. The ten *sefirot*, or spheres, structure the divine universe.
Humans can access this universe primarily through visionary
experience. Although the dates of primary texts like the *Zohar* and
the *Sefer Yezirah* remain in discussion, the mystical and visionary
concepts that underlie them offer a different approach to divine
understanding than the philosophies of writers like Moses Maimonides (1135–1204), who, like Ibn-Rushd an Ibn-Sina, combined
theology with Aristotelian principles. A doctor, *talmud* commentator,
and biblical scholar, Maimonides' work spread widely throughout
and beyond the Jewish community. His best-known work, *The
Guide to the Perplexed*, made extensive use of scholastic philosophy
and employed a "negative theology," or a description of things,
particularly God, by what they are not. He is also known for
constructing the Thirteen Attributes of God, also called the Thirteen
Principles of Faith. Although he expressed a form of intellectual
mysticism, he was an opponent of poetry, finding it inherently false
and founded on invention, not truth.

CONCLUSION

The function of religion in the literature of the Middle Ages cannot
be underestimated, but assuming that presence to be monolithic is
to undersell the wide range of spiritual material produced during
the period. Medieval religious literature is highly diverse in its forms,
in its assumptions, and in its relation to the religious authority of
the period. It also has a vast spectrum in its relationship to the

secular world; a text like the *Ancrene Wisse* can draw language, metaphor, and inspiration from courtly romance while simultaneously rejecting the secular world that produced those texts, while Dante's *Divine Comedy* (see Chapter 6) can be both a theological and a political document at the same time. To consider the period entirely Christian is to miss the powerful literary expressions produced in the Jewish and Islamic worlds, and it risks reducing medieval religious literature to a univalent body of work expressing a single theme. More broadly, one should consider works like the Old Norse *Prose Edda* (extant in a 13th-century manuscript) or the *Saga of the Volusngs* (also 13th century) that pre-date the arrival of Christianity in Scandinavia, and even *Beowulf*, which provide evidence of European paganism and express a different, more fatalistic religious message that widens the scope and ways in which the literature of the Middle Ages touches heaven.

FOR FURTHER READING

PRIMARY TEXTS

The large collection of works listed here shows the range and diversity of religious literary expression in the Middle Ages. Because these two texts are often considered foundations for much of the religious literature of the period, readers might well begin with **Augustine of Hippo's (2008). *Confessions*. Trans. Garry Wills. London: Penguin** and **Boethius. (2000). *The Consolation of Philosophy*. Trans. Victor Watts. London: Penguin**. Vestiges of these works can be found in much of the Christian writing throughout the period. For a background on anchoritic spirituality, readers might begin with the ***Ancrene Wisse: A Guide for Anchoresses*. (1994). Trans. Hugh White. London: Penguin**, and for monasticism, ***The Rule of St. Benedict* (1981). Ed. Timothy Fry, Timothy Horner, and Imogen Baker. Collegeville, MN: Liturgical Press** offers an often pithy introduction to how monks governed themselves with some surprises that challenge views of what the enclosed life was like.

The essential collection of hagiographies was **Jacobus de Voragine. (1999). *The Golden Legend: Selections*. Trans. Christopher Stace. London: Penguin**, which influenced saints' lives throughout the period. The mystical tradition, which formed such a large body of medieval religious literature is well represented: **Hildegarde of Bingen. (2001).** *Selected Writings.* **Trans. Mark Atherton. London: Penguin** (from early in the period); **Julian of Norwich. (1999).** *Revelations of Divine Love.* **Trans. Elizabeth Spearing. London: Penguin** (from the later Middle Ages); and **Margery Kempe. (2005).** *The Book of Margery Kempe.* **Ed. and Trans. Barry Windeatt. London: Penguin.** Hildegard and Julian write from within the monastic and anchoritic traditions, while Margery Kempe shows the mystical experiences of a layperson outside the official Church.

The drama of Hrotsvit, which uses classical roman comedy to tell religious stories, can be found in *Hrotsvit of Gandersheim: A Florilegium of her Works.* **(1998). Ed. and Trans. Katherina M. Wilson. Cambridge: D. S. Brewer.** Cycle Drama, one of the Middle Ages' strongest performative traditions, is well represented by *The Wakefield Mystery Plays: A Selection.* **(1969). Ed. Marshall Rose. New York: W. W. Norton.** This cycle contains several well-known and very rewarding plays. The dream vision is a very popular medieval form; one of the most extended examples is **William Langland. (2009).** *The Vision of Piers the Plowman: A New Translation of the B-Text.* **Ed. and Trans. A. V. C. Schmidt. Oxford: Oxford University Press.** Those interested in the stories of the Norse tradition can find their origins in **Snorri Sturluson. (2005).** *The Prose Edda.* **Trans. Jesse Byock. London: Penguin.**

The medieval religious poet who enjoys the most continuous popularity today is **Jalaloddin Rumi. (2007).** *Spiritual Verses.* **Ed. and Trans. Alan Williams. London: Penguin**; his spiritual inquiry can be balanced against **Moses Maimonides. (1956).** *A Guide to the Perplexed.* **Trans. M. Friedlander. New York: Dover**, one of the representatives of the intellectual religious tradition that develops in the twelfth century, leading it to be known as the Twelfth-Century Renaissance.

SECONDARY SOURCES

An excellent resource that gives a broad perspective on medieval religion is *Medieval Religion: New Resources* **(2005). Ed. Constance Hoffman Berman. London: Routledge**, which offers a series of articles by important scholars taking interesting approaches to the subject. **Karen Louise Jolly's (1996).** *Tradition and Diversity: Christianity in a World Context to 1500.* **London: Routledge** provides an historical and broadly-geographical background. **Elizabeth Avilda Petroff's (1994).** *Body and Soul: Essays on Medieval Women and Mysticism.* **Oxford: Oxford University Press** opens a window into the world of mystical women's writing and its intersections with hagiographical writing. **Peter Brown's (2014).** *The Cult of the Saints: Its Rise and Function in Latin Christianity.* **Chicago: University of Chicago Press** explores the veneration of saints, and in particular their remains, and how it became a central focus of medieval devotional practice. For those interested in the monastic system which produced many of the medieval writers discussed above, **C. H. Lawrence's (2015)** *Medieval Monasticism: Forms of Religious Life in Western Europe in the Middle Ages.* **London: Routledge** offers extensive background. **David Nirenberg's (2014).** *Neighboring Faiths: Christianity, Islam, and Judaism in the Middle Ages and Today.* **Chicago: University of Chicago Press** examines how the three faiths interacted, encountered, and thought about each other in the medieval period and considers the implications of those connections for the world today. **Rosalind and Christopher Brooke's (1984).** *Popular Religion in the Middle Ages: Western Europe 1000–1300.* **London: Thames and Hudson** gives insight into popular religious practices, many of which inform medieval religious writing. Less directly related to the literature, but truly fascinating are **Patrick Geary's (1991).** *Furta Sacra: Thefts of Relics in the Central Middle Ages.* **Princeton, NJ: Princeton University Press**, which shows how the value of sacred body parts led to the plundering of churches, raiding of tombs, and looting of catacombs, often by clerics and churchmen, and **Carolyn Walker Bynum's (1988)** *Holy Feast, Holy Fast: The Significance of Food to Religious Women.* **Berkeley, CA: University of California Press** explores the function of food, and in particular starvation, in the elevation and ultimately veneration of religious women from 1200–1500. While most of these works are not directly about the religious writers listed in the *Primary Texts* section, they provide truly valuable background for understanding and interpreting those texts whose underlying assumptions may be opaque to modern readers.

5

MEETING MONSTERS ON THE MAP

MEDIEVAL LITERATURE OF SPACE AND TIME

INTRODUCTION

In *Maps of the Imagination: The Writer as Cartographer*, Peter Turchi evocatively says: "To ask for a map is to say, 'tell me a story'" (Turchi 2004: 11). He might well be talking about a medieval map, which even more than others presents real, geographic space in a fictional mode more driven by ideology than by accuracy. One of the Middle Ages' most famous maps, the Hereford Mappamundi, creates its own universe with God and the angels above and humans exploring and making maps below; the very act of its own making is incorporated into the map. The earthly world shows cities and towns and rivers but also fantastical creatures and figures from myth and history. In Asia, a pelican feeds its young from its own breast, and in Samarkand, a Cicone with a bird-head sits beside the Oxus river. Issedones eat the corpses of their parents next to the Golden Fleece. The blurring of the geographical and the fictional creates a universe built of both space and narrative; locations and their stories are simultaneously represented. In addition, these maps evoke a series of different histories in showing what Chet Van Duzer calls a "geography of the marvelous" (Van Duzer 2013: 10).

Maps also represent Christian history, connecting the real and the transcendent in a visual form; the medieval T-O formation, the T standing for the Cross and the O for the world, with Jerusalem at the center, creates a narrative of the world subservient to God and narrating the story of salvation. Lisa Deam comments that medieval maps move from "world to worldview" (Deam 2015: 12). These same worlds and worldviews are represented in the medieval literature of place, whether through the blending of place and narrative in travel narratives, the journey of the soul to God that underlies the narratives of pilgrimage, or the association of real places with histories both literal and fantastic in the historiographies and chronicles.

One of the challenges of writing about medieval literature is covering fairly vast constitutions of space and time; this chapter seeks to consider how medieval literature itself dealt with questions of geography and history through an exploration of travelogues, historiographies, and chronicles. National identity, to the extent such a thing existed, emerges in the Middle Ages in histories, such as Geoffrey of Monmouth's *History of the Kings of Britain* (1137) or the Old Norse *Vinland Sagas* (13th century), which both narrate and validate the presence of particular people in particular places. That said, interactions between peoples – both conflict and encounter – are often documented in chronicle romances, which build narrative from historical moments, such as the Crusades; a comparison of *King Richard the Lionhearted* (14th century), and Froissart's *Chronicles* (14th century) shows how history and fiction interact with each other in a medieval mode. Travelogues such as *The Travels of Sir John Mandeville* (c. 1357–71), the voyages of Marco Polo (1254–1324) or Ibn-Battuta (1304–68), and texts like *The Marvels of the East* (c. 1100) show how medieval peoples understood each other (or didn't understand each other), and how they conceived of their geographical world as well as their historical one.

TRAVEL NARRATIVES

The range of medieval attitudes towards travel and encounter might well be represented by examples from two of the best-known European travelogues from the period, *The Travels of Sir John Mandeville* and Marco Polo's *Description of the World*, also called *Travels*. Of the Nicobar Islands, Mandeville says:

> Thence one travels by sea to another land, called Natumeran [Nicobar Islands]. It is a large and a fair island, whose circuit is nearly a

thousand miles. Men and women of that isle have heads like dogs, and they are called Cynocephales. These people, despite their shape, are fully reasonable and intelligent. They worship an ox as their god. Each one of them carries an ox made of gold or silver on his brow, as a token that they love their god well. They go quite naked expect for a little cloth around their privy parts. They are big in stature and good warriors; they carry a large shield, which covers their body, and a long spear in their hand, and dressed in this way they go boldly against their enemies. If they capture any man in battle, they eat him. The king of that land is a great and mighty lord, rich, and very devout according to his creed.

(Mandeville 2005: 134)

Marco Polo tells the story a bit differently, however:

When one leaves Java and the kingdom of Lambri and he goes north about 150 miles, then one finds 2 islands, one of which is called Nicobar. On this island they have no king and are like animals and I tell you that they go around completely naked, males and females, and don't cover themselves with anything in the world; they are idolators. I tell you that all their woods are of noble trees of great worth: they are red sandal, Indian nuts, clove, brazilwood, and many other good trees.

There is nothing else worth mentioning; for this we will leave and will tell you about the other island, called Andaman.

(Polo 2016: 155)

Mandeville's fascination with the marvelous and Polo's interest in goods and trade emerge from these descriptions, although neither is the most representative of those impulses in the text. However, the Cynocephales and the other marvelous humans Mandeville sees – Blemi with their heads in their chests and people with one leg so large they can use it as an umbrella to shield them from the sun while hopping about on the other – suggest that his goal in travel is to see difference, to see marvels and spectacles and magical places. His travels end in the lands of the magical Prester John, a Christian Emperor in control of many lands lost among the lands of the Muslims and others; therefore, his journey seems to move from the familiar to the exotic, increasingly shifting from what might be recognizable into fantasy. While scholars have been interested in whether the person who calls himself Sir John Mandeville (itself a fantasy, since the *Travels* appears to have been written by someone else, and no Knight called John Mandeville appears to have existed) actually traveled to any of the places he claims to experience; it is clear that by the time he moves past the Middle East, he's in the realm of the imaginary. Drawing from works like the Old English *Marvels* (or *Wonders) of the East*, found in three manuscripts including the *Beowulf* manuscript and other examples of the *Mirabila* tradition – letters or travelogues about encounters with exotic creatures and miraculous places – Mandeville's engagement is not primarily with reality, but with its opposite. While in earlier sections, he finds similarity between himself and the Islamic inhabitants of the Middle East, and often says they are more diligent and devoted in the practice of their (wrong) religion than many Christians are in theirs, he very quickly ceases to see much in common with what he observes in his travels.

Marco Polo, on the other hand, despite his work sometimes being called *The Book of the Marvels of the World*, seems much more interested in seeing what is available for trade. Written down by Rustichello of Pisa, a writer of romances who met Marco Polo in prison, these *Travels* seem driven by different impulses than Mandeville's. His mercantile sentiment causes him to focus on similarities between people rather than differences. Although he likes a good magical site as much as anyone else, he seems to reduce a great deal of his observation to a kind of formula, which may be exemplified by his description of Quilon, southwest of Malabar:

> Quilon is a kingdom one finds toward the southwest, when one leaves Malabar and has gone 500 miles. They are idolaters; there are also Christians and Jews. They have their own language; the king pays tribute to no one. Now I want to tell you what is found in this kingdom and what grows there.
>
> (Polo 2016: 172)

In Polo's view, people share inherent similarities – they have a religion and a language, they eat products native to their region, and they produce things valuable for trade. Their religions and languages may differ from Polo's own, but while he will sometimes iterate a custom he finds particularly different or intriguing, his primary sense seems to be that people do the same things everywhere, but what's most exciting is the goods and products they make. Polo's tales end in China, and while he was not the first Westerner to get there, and while there remains scholarly discussion about where he actually went or whether he went there at all, it is clear that his purpose in narrating the story was different from Mandeville's. Certainly, many of his observations have been verified, such as the presence of Nestorian Christian churches in Zhenjiang, methods of salt production, and specific details of the currency used in the region. Instead of enumerating fantastic marvels, particularly those closer to home, he often debunks them, and instead of seeing Blemi and Cynocephales, he tends to see people who look like himself. Franciscan Friar and Traveller Odoric of Pordenone (1286–1331) described many marvelous races in his visits to China, including tiny pygmies, people with no joints in their legs, and women who married dogs. Polo seems to view the Chinese as simply another group of people with their own language, religion, government, food, and goods. Whether he went there or not, his perspective on travel seems to value the real (or realistic, at least) and the commercial over the fantastic.

Marco Polo is far more famous than his book; he is widely talked about as an explorer and tradesman, credited with bringing noodles to Italy (a story given little credence by Italians). The eponymous two-season television show (2014–15), staring Lorenzo Richelmy as Marco Polo and Benedict Wong as Kublai Khan, featured very little detail from the book, instead inventing a variety of romances and intrigues, although it did receive an award from the President of Mongolia, Tshakhiagiin Elbegdoj, for its depiction of the Mongolian people.

Both of these specific accounts, and the two traditions they represent, had great currency in their time. Christopher Columbus, as he set out to discover a new route to India in 1492, had both Mandeville's and Marco Polo's texts on board.

Other travelers more interested in providing a comprehensive account of a very human world include Ibn-Battuta, the widest-ranging Islamic traveler, whose narrative, the *Rihla* or *Travels*, ranges across the entire Muslim world, and who also may have traveled to China. While scholars have concluded that he also did not visit everywhere he claimed and relied on a long history of Islamic travel to create many of his descriptions, it seems clear that he did cover a sizable portion of the distance he describes, and that he also seemed more interested in tracing the spread of his own religion than in seeing marvels and exotics. His descriptions of oddities can be very literal, such as his description of the rhinoceros – "It is smaller than an elephant but its head is many times larger than an elephant's. It has a single horn between its eyes, about three cubits in length and about a span in breadth" (Ibn-Battuta 2002: 151) – or more fantastic, as in his description of the ruins at Tarna:

> Ala al-Mulk told me that the historians assert that in this place there was a great city whose inhabitants were so given to depravity that they turned to stone, and that is their king who is on the platform in the house we have described, which is still called the 'king's palace.'
>
> (Ibn-Battuta 2002: 154)

In China, Ibn-Battuta was unimpressed with the country because of the paganism practiced by most people, but he was still engaged by the various objects available for trade and the beauty of the place, showing a mercantile interest similar to Marco Polo's. In the tenth century, Ahmad Ibn Fadlān, who traveled as a member of an embassy of the Abbasid Caliph of Baghdad to the ruler of the Volga Bulgars, wrote an account of his journeys known as the *Risala*, which details both the routes he took and the people he encountered on the way – chief among the marvels he witnesses are the northern lights. Although he is primarily interested in the spread of Islam, his work has become known for his account of the Vikings he called the Rus, who he found to be perfect physical specimens, if somewhat remiss in their hygiene. Describing the people and their customs, he also witnessed a Viking ship burial, whose account has much in common with both textual descriptions from Scandinavian works and archeological evidence of ship burials found in Norway and in England at Sutton Hoo. Ibn Fadlān's travels were the inspiration for Michael Crichton's novel *Eaters of the Dead* (1976) and the subsequent film *The Thirteenth Warrior* (1999).

Preceding Marco Polo by a century, Jewish traveler Benjamin of Tudela (1130–73) visited Africa, Asia, and Europe. With a strong knowledge of languages and an abiding interest in cartography, he provided a demographic account of Jewish communities throughout the region and expressed a continuing interest in the gem, particularly coral, trade, in his *Travels*. His accounts of urban populations, Jewish and non-Jewish, and his descriptions of local customs were noted for their accuracy, in particular because unlike many of his compatriots, he cited his sources.

Other travelers stayed closer to home, although their encounters with local cultures different from their own were often very dramatic. Willibald's eighth-century *Life of St. Boniface* narrates a journey whose dual purposes were sanctity and conversion. The actions of English cleric St. Boniface (c. 675–754) led to his canonization and the conversion of many in the Germania (a region encompassing a swathe of Germanic Central Europe, named by the Roman Empire). Observations about particular places are tied primarily to Boniface's successes, for example, his daring choice to cut down a sacred pagan oak tree:

> With the counsel and advice of the latter persons, Boniface in their presence attempted to cut down, at a place called Gaesmere, a certain oak of extraordinary size called in the old tongue of the pagans the Oak of Jupiter. Taking his courage in his hands (for a great crowd of pagans stood by watching and bitterly cursing in their hearts the enemy of the gods), he cut the first notch. But when he had made a superficial cut, suddenly, the oak's vast bulk, shaken by a mighty blast of wind from above crashed to the ground shivering its topmost branches into fragments in its fall. As if by the express will of God (for the brethren present had done nothing to cause it) the oak burst asunder into four parts, each part having a trunk of equal length. At the sight of this extraordinary spectacle the heathens who had been cursing ceased to revile and began, on the contrary, to believe and bless the Lord. Thereupon the holy bishop took counsel with the brethren, built an oratory from the timber of the oak and dedicated it to Saint Peter the Apostle. He then set out on a journey to Thuringia, having accomplished by the help of God all the things we have already mentioned. Arrived there, he addressed the elders and the chiefs of the people, calling on them to put aside their blind ignorance and to return to the Christian religion that they had formerly embraced.
>
> (Willibald 1916: section 6)

Unlike his fellow travelers interested in exotica, Boniface's goals seem not to be to observe but to alter. By turning the oak tree into a church, Boniface both expanded the Christian corpora and made the strange and exotic into the familiar. While earlier than any of the works mentioned above, Boniface may offer the most interesting blend of the two approaches.

These are by no means the only medieval travelers who wrote about their experiences; they simply stand out as examples of the varying ways in which these travelers experienced the world around them and the people they encountered, and the texts provide a window into what they saw and wanted to see. All medieval travelers give a sense of a world potentially extraordinary and potentially comfortable; Ibn-Battuta may not have found China conducive, but he was delighted by the warm welcomes he received from fellow Muslims there; Marco Polo may have found the ghosts of the dessert of Lop fascinating, but he is ultimately more engaged by methods of preserving fruit.

The most common form of medieval travel, and the one open to the largest percentage of the populace, was pilgrimage. As a journey, it was both literal and symbolic; in traveling to a local shrine or more far afield to Santiago de Compostela or Jerusalem, the pilgrim enacted the journey from birth to salvation, from the earthly present to the Heavenly Jerusalem. However, while enacting it, the pilgrim also faced arduous and lengthy travel, whether over land or across the sea. Pilgrimage offered a combination of "danger, adventure, and curiosity," as Donald Howard notes in *Writers and Pilgrims* (Howard 1980: 14). Travel was time-consuming and took pilgrims out of their everyday lives, exposing them to a range of experiences, mundane and revelatory, from disgusting local foods and souvenirs in the form of pilgrim badges to truly transcendent experiences at the shrines themselves.

The large body of pilgrimage literature – guidebooks, journals, narratives – is, then, hardly surprising; Howard notes, "it was not surprising that writers wrote books about such a popular institution. More – many more – were written about the pilgrimage than about comparable medieval institutions" (1980: 16). Often religious and moral, these also attempted to create the pilgrimage experience vicariously for their readers. Some of the best known include French canon Jacques de Vitry's *History of Jerusalem* (1180) and German Dominican Wilhelm von Boldensele's *Itinerarium* (1285–1338/9);

pilgrimage narratives are included in the *Book of Margery Kempe* and of course Chaucer's *Canterbury Tales*; Dante's *Divine Comedy* is a pilgrimage, and some of his unique modes and challenges of travel are exaggerations of the challenges real pilgrims faced on the roads to Walsingham, Canterbury, Santiago, and the Holy Land. In Boldensele's book, besides offering useful routes and suggestions for travel, he describes everything notable he sees, including bananas, elephants, pyramids, and tombs; the journey is just as interesting, perhaps more so, than the destination.

HISTORIOGRAPHIES, HISTORIES, AND CHRONICLES

While all the narratives above share a movement through space, medieval writers were equally interested in chronicling a particular space through time. More than just sources for medieval history, these works of historiography have political and social functions: they can be didactic and moral; they often believe that history is guided by divine providence; as much as the travel narratives discussed above, they readily accept the marvelous and miraculous as part of the history of a place or family.

Geoffrey of Monmouth, in the *Historia Regum Britaniae*, traces British history back to Brutus, a Trojan who survived the war and then set out, landing in Britain and naming the Island after himself; one of his followers, Corineus, went South and named Cornwall after himself. Once there, he wrestled repeatedly with the giants who inhabited the land. All but one giant, Gogmagog, were conquered by the Britons, but Brutus kept Gogmagog alive so as to see a wrestling match between him and Corineus. Finally overcoming the giant's strength, Corineus:

> heaved Gogmagog up on to his shoulders, and running as fast as he could under the weight, he hurried off to the nearby coast. He clambered up to the top of a mighty cliff, shook himself free and hurled this deadly monster, whom he was carrying on his shoulders, far out into the sea. The giant fell on to a sharp reef of rocks, where he was dashed into a thousand fragments and stained the waters with his blood. The place took its name from the fact that the giant was hurled down there and it is called Gogmagog's Leap to this day.
>
> (1966: 73)

Geoffrey's temporal narrative is infused with stories about places, whether establishing their names, as above, or their importance. A narrative about the Roman invasion of Britain gives way to the Prophesies of Merlin and one of the earliest detailed, extended narratives of King Arthur, and finally the invasion of the Angles and Saxons. Geoffrey's political opinions are very clear; as a post-Norman Conquest writer (his own origins, despite his naming his ties to Monmouth, are somewhat unclear – he may be Welsh, or from a Breton family that came with William during the Conquest), his desire is to establish a history of Britain connecting the Britons to the land well before 1066, and showing the Anglo-Saxon period as the low-point of the Island's history. As such, he legitimates the current rulers of the country by claiming for them a lengthy and miraculous narrative.

Critical of Geoffrey was his Welsh compatriot, Gerald of Wales (c. 1146 – c. 1223), who found the *Historia* too full of marvels to be believed. His own works, however, show many of the same impulses, although they are more map driven. The *Topographica Hibernica* [The Topography of Ireland] (1188) and the *Descriptio Cambriae* [Description of Wales] (1194) both consider landscape, flora, fauna, place names, and history but they are not devoid of miraculous and marvelous stores either – in the *Topographica Hibernica* Gerald tells the story of a priest who has a lengthy encounter with two Ossory werewolves, who had been cursed by Abbot Natalis to withdraw from human habitation and take on the forms of wolves. If they survive, they can return home and are replaced with two new werewolves. The female werewolf is very ill; the priest gives her last rites and removes her werewolf skin, showing her to be a human underneath. After receiving communion, her companion pulls her skin back up, and they return to their werewolf existence, which leads Gerald to meditate on Augustine's discussion of werewolves and metamorphosis in *City of God*, which says that metamorphosis can only take place externally through divine intervention, and that it is an illustrative illusion. This episode has been read as a condemnation of the Irish as bestial, but still human and redeemable through the sacraments, which would justify their conquering by the Normans (Karkov 2003: 95). The *Descriptio Cambriae* seems particularly interested in considering how the Welsh might be brought to submission; Gerald believes their angry natures can be monetized by pitting them against each other. Gerald may disagree with Geoffrey's methodology, but they share more than they diverge, including a political conviction in the right of the Normans to rule Britain.

Other chroniclers, like Bede in the *Historia Ecclesiastica Gentis Anglorum* [History of the English Church and People] (731) and Jean Froissart (c. 1337 – c. 1405) in his *Chronicles* seem more interested in presenting history without the miraculous. Bede's focus on the Christianization of England during the Anglo-Saxon period, from Roman Britain to his own time, leans towards actual events and theological conflicts, such as the dating of Easter. It does contain poetic moments, including the story of Caedmon (who avoids feasts and celebrations because he can't sing), who, hiding in the sheepfold, is called upon by God to sing Him a hymn about Creation and thus creates the first Old English poem.

Froissart's narration of a particular part of the Hundred-Years War (c. 1326–1400) includes lively depictions of warfare and an examination of chivalric culture at the end of the period, incorporating events such as King Charles V's coronation (1380), and in 1389, the marriage of John, Duke of Berry and Jeanne de Boulogne, and the entry of the French queen Isabeau of Bavaria into Paris. Covering events from England to Western Europe to North Africa, and explaining a great deal about military strategy, preparation for war, and the battles themselves, Froissart provides a broad portrait of an extended conflict at a particular time. Like Geoffrey and Gerald, his political leanings are clear – there is no attempt at neutrality in a medieval chronicle.

Various forms of chronicles exist from nearly every region during the medieval period; some are focused specifically on local history, such as the *Anglo-Saxon Chronicle* (9th century), which narrates Old English history from the exit of the Romans to the moment of its writing. Although many stories are contradictory and its biases are foregrounded, it remains one of the key sources of knowledge about the period. Latin chronicles detail histories of monastic houses, such as Jocelin of Brakelond's *Chronicle of the Abbey of Bury St. Edmunds* (12th century), providing insight into the life of a medieval religious community. Religious histories include *inventios* and *translatios* – stories about the origins of particular communities, often grounded in miracles or visions from saints making claims on particular pieces of property on which the foundations were based. When these stories involve the discovery of relics, the narratives include the bringing of the relic to its rightful place in the monastic house, again often incorporating miraculous stories of their finding, such as relics that speak (or, at least, become a kind of mouthpiece on earth for the saint in heaven) calling the monks to their location to unearth them or reclaim them from a different (and apparently incorrect) monastery and bring them to their rightful place.

Vernacular chronicles trace the lineages of Royal Families or the deeds of kings, such as Jean de Joinville's *Life of St. Louis, King of France* (1309), a biography of the King and an account of the Seventh Crusade. Some trace history from Biblical times to the present, incorporating human and spiritual history, such as Hartmann Schedel's richly illustrated *Nuremberg Chronicle* (1493). From the beginning to the end of the period, chroniclers attempted to preserve what they thought was important to remember for posterity; in so doing, they preserved factual evidence, local stories, and oral histories, and, perhaps most important for literary interest, habits of mind and ideas about narrative importance. While the chronicles have always been of significant interest to medieval historians, in their narrative choices, incorporation of stories, stylistics, and engagement with their audiences they are often fruitful for exploration by scholars of literature as well.

SAGAS

Although we have discussed the Icelandic sagas in some length in Chapter 2, focusing on the violence at the core of these narratives, it is also worth noting here that many of the sagas are also chronicles, blending fact and fiction in their narration of the establishment of populations in Iceland, Greenland, the Orkney Islands, and North America. Even sagas seemingly disconnected from specific places tell the stories of particular families; the *Volsunga Saga* [Saga of the Volsungs] (13th century) narrates the origin and decline of the Volsungs. The saga includes marvels like werewolves and talking dragons, sorceresses, spells, and forgetting potions, and Odin appears repeatedly at the margins of the story influencing its outcome, but it also includes historical figures including Atilla the Hun and events such as the destruction of the Burgundians in the fifth century. Thematically it examines the simultaneous necessity for and destructive nature of revenge, masculine and feminine behavior, and the need for punishment of wrongs. In the preserved manuscript version, another theme emerges from its own temporal moment – the ways in which a tribal society is altered by the influence of outside trends, in this case represented by continental literature in the form of the romance.

More typical sagas tell dramatic narratives overlaid on a history of a particular place. One less-read tale, the *Orkneyinga Saga* [Saga of the Earls of Orkney] (c. 1230), tells the story of the three-century earlier conquest of the Orkney Islands by the Norse under King Harald Fairhair. The saga, like many of the medieval historiographic works, blends mythology, history, legend, and truth. Against a somewhat mythic background, the saga considers issues of taxation of farmers, how one becomes an earl and what happens when two nobles claim the title at once, and the power of absentee kings. Adding two other forms of narrative, the text combines Earl Rognvald's pilgrimage to Jerusalem and Constantinople with a travel narrative. Far more fascinating than the pilgrimage itself, the journey includes a romance with the Queen of Narbonne, the freeing of Galician natives from an oppressive Lord, a stunning act of piracy in the Straits of Gibraltar, a description of the sites in the Holy Land, and a great deal of route information about how to get from place to place.

The Eyrbygga Saga (13th century) is more distinctly tied to a place, primarily the Snæfellsnes peninsula, but in tracing the community's founding and the establishment of the families there, it records a great deal of pagan ritual, practice, and belief at the time of the conversion to Christianity. The tension between the two religions can be seen in the death of Thoraguna, a rich woman and reader of signs, who foretells her own death and insists that she must be taken to Skàlholt (the seat of the first Icelandic bishop) because it will soon be a highly venerated place, where priests will sing Mass for her soul. The blending of Christian and Pagan before her death only amplifies on the journey to Skàlhot, where she rises naked from her coffin to take provisions and cook dinner for the travelers when they're treated ungenerously by the farmer with whom they lodge on the way. Bad omens on the way home, despite an easy journey, presage deaths, and indeed people begin dying and a seal ghost starts appearing. These dark forces all seem to be caused by their failure to dispose of Thoraguna's bed in the way she desired; indeed, the seal ghost, the saga implies, is Thoraguna. Simultaneously an avowed Christian and a pagan ghost, Thoraguna embodies the blended qualities of this saga, which, like the others discussed here, incorporates into its history of transition from Norway to Iceland and paganism to Christianity, a powerful body of legend and myth.

Most sagas incorporate stories of marvels into their histories of places and peoples. The *Vinland Sagas*, consisting of two independent works written in the thirteenth century – *Eirík's Saga Rauða* [Erik the Red's Saga] and *Grænlendinga Saga* [The Saga of The Greenlanders] – both contain accounts of the Norse voyages to North America, which they called "Vinland" [Wineland] because they apparently discovered grapevines there. Offering the most complete information about the travels of Lief Eiriksson, they include information about the goods and natural resources they found there as well as conflict with the local Native American population, whom they called "*skraelings*" [foreigners]. At first these relationships were relatively cordial, and they traded freely – exchanging dairy products for furs – though they eventually turned hostile, which led the Norse to return to Greenland and make no further journeys. Although lighter on marvels than some of the other sagas, the stories of exploration remain balanced with descriptions of exotic goods and one notable encounter between Guðrið and a Native American woman. Although textual notes often give this exchange a logical explanation, the text presents it as a supernatural event, although with the same *laissez-faire* that these kinds of events receive in all the sagas. Although the *Vinland Sagas* are not entirely historically accurate, and indeed the two contradict each other in places, they do provide substantial evidence of Norse exploration of North America, which led to archeologist Anne Stine Ingstad and explorer Helge Ingstad to locate and excavate the Viking Era settlement at L'Anse aux Meadows in Newfoundland, Canada in the 1960s. The site, which includes a reconstruction of a medieval Viking longhouse, is now a UNESCO World Heritage Site.

CONCLUSION

Geraldine Heng, in *Empire of Magic*, comments about Geoffrey of Monmouth that his "story is remarkable for many exemplary demonstrations: chief of which perhaps is how, in a resourcefully accommodating cultural medium, historical phenomena and fantasy may collide and vanish, each into each other, without explanation or apology, at the precise locations where both can be readily mined to best advantage" (Heng 2003: 2). In this description, she encapsulates medieval literature of time and space. The incorporation of mythology, legend, marvel, and miracle into what is essentially an attempt to construct history provides an incorporation not just of events but also of cultural desires and interests, an insight into the complex ways people thought, perhaps what we might call a melding of history and literature. While the forms differ, the travelogue, historiography, chronicle, and saga, in their attempts to engage with the temporal and the geographic, all find themselves incorporating the literal and the fantastic. Engaging political, social, and religious questions, these narratives are at the source of the creation of many contemporary ideas about nation, collective identity, political relationships, and social behavior. Some of these, such as nationalism and race, have developed through varying prioritizing discourses into the dangerous forms in which we encounter them today. And yet, the medieval versions do often suggest more potential than the discourses that have emerged from them; Ibn Fadlān may find the Rus disgusting in their personal habits, but he can still see a beauty in them, and Sir John Mandeville can praise the Egyptians for their devotion to their faith and the sincerity of their worship, even if he ultimately says the faith and worship is wrong. That two travelers can essentially encounter each other's people and find the same balance of admiration and critique shows how little force any single totalizing narrative can really hold, and reminds readers that all stories have multiple sides and represent multiple voices. Like the medieval map, which situated sea monsters and magical creatures in historical places, and built a visual connection between human and transcendent history, these narratives suggest how "reality" and fiction combine to produce varying kinds of ideologies. The cliché that the present cannot be understood without the past is given some shape here; these narratives, however, suggest the advantages of paying a new visit to the past to see how complexly it truly constructs its own story.

FOR FURTHER READING

PRIMARY TEXTS

For those who would like to travel with these medieval travelers, the rewards of reading these texts are significant. Marco Polo is often considered the standard, given his wide-reaching influence, although he can sometimes seem repetitive to a modern reader: **Marco Polo (2016). *The Description of the World*. Ed. and Trans. Sharon Kinoshita. Indianapolis, IN: Hackett Publishing**. Sir John Mandeville, being more intrigued by marvels, alphabets, and peculiarities, offers more pleasures, if less sense of what the medieval world was actually like: ***The Travels of Sir John Mandeville* (2005). Ed. and Trans. C. W. R. D. Moseley. London: Penguin**. Ibn-Fadlān is mostly given attention for his descriptions of the Rus, or Vikings, in the North, although his travels to that point, and his experiences of preparing for cold weather, are also fascinating: **Ibn-Fadlān (2012). *Ibn Fadlān and the Land of Darkness: Arab Travellers in the Far North*. London: Penguin** includes not just Ibn-Fadlān's adventures but also those of several other Arabic travelers who traveled well beyond Islamic-controlled lands, including additional meetings with Vikings. ***The Travels of Ibn Battutah* (2002). Ed. and Trans. Tim Mackintosh-Smith. London: Picador** offers a detailed and varied picture of medieval civilization as well as some interesting comparisons to Marco Polo and Mandeville as they visit some of the same places in the Indian subcontinent. The adventures of Jewish medieval travelers are compiled in ***Jewish Travellers in the Middle Ages: 19 Firsthand Accounts* (1987). Ed. Elkan Nathan Adler from the Translation by J. D. Eisenstein. New York: Dover**, offering perspectives on the Middle East, Europe, and North Africa.

For those more interested in how medieval writers construct the histories of their homelands, a good place to begin is with **Bede (2003). *An Ecclesiastical History of the English People*. Ed. D. Farmer and Trans. Leo Sherley-Price. London: Penguin**, a story of the Anglo-Saxon conquest and development in England; this story is framed differently by **Geoffrey of Monmouth (1966).** *The History of the Kings of Britain.* **Trans. Lewis Thorpe. London: Penguin**. Geoffrey's history goes all the way back to the Trojan War and fits the story of King Arthur into his broad sweep of the Island's history. **Jean Froissart (1978).** *Chronicles.* **Ed. and Trans. Geoffrey Brereton. London: Penguin** provides a similar, if less magical, history of France, with a vivid focus on the Hundred-Years War. Unfortunately, Hartman Schedel's *Nuremberg Chronicle* seem hard to come by in remotely affordable English versions, although ***Medieval Woodcut Illustrations: City Views and Decorations from the Nuremberg Chronicle* (1998). Ed. Carol Belanger Grafton. New York: Dover** does provide an opportunity to see some of the richness of one of the versions, and in the spirit of this chapter, if not the medium, how the medieval world views itself. For a more micro-focus, readers might enjoy **Jocelin of Brakelond (1989).** *Chronicle of the Abbey of Bury St. Edmunds.* **Ed. and Trans. Diana Greenway and Jane Sayers. Oxford: Oxford University Press**, which looks at the development of one foundation at one time.

Readers interested in the Icelandic material will enjoy *The Saga of the Volsungs.* **(2004). Ed. and Trans. Jesse L. Byock. London: Penguin**, which tells the story of the rise and fall of the Volsung Family in the fourth and fifth centuries. For stories about the foundations of communities in Iceland, the comprehensive volume, *The Sagas of the Icelanders* **(2001). Ed. Robert Kellog with multiple translators. London: Penguin**, offers a broad range of the available narratives, including the *Saga of the People of Laxardal* and the *Vinland Sagas*; one example that it does not include, *Eyrbygga Saga* **(1989). Trans. Hermann Palsson and Paul Edwards. London: Penguin**, shows in particular the effects of the conversion to Christianity on a national scale.

SECONDARY SOURCES

The integration of economies through trade and exchange saw a large movement of people with different agendas – pilgrims, diplomats, merchants, missionaries, and adventurers; despite the difficulties and expense of travel, the sheer volume of narratives about these experiences suggest a new concept of human mobility explored in **Shayne Aaron Legassie (2017).** *The Invention of Medieval Travel.* These intersections of peoples in the Middle Ages which are revealed in the travelogues are discussed in a variety of important ways in medieval scholarship. Focusing on medieval Spain, a place where people of many religions cohabitated successfully, is **Maria Rosa Menocal (2002).** *Ornament of the World: How Muslims, Jews, and Christians Created a Culture of Tolerance in Medieval Spain.* **Boston: Little, Brown.** To consider the ways in which the West viewed the East, some of this constructed by the very travelers discussed in this chapter, see **Suzanne Conklin Akbari (2009).** *Idols of the East: European Representations of Islam and the Orient, 1100–1450.* **Ithaca, NY: Cornell University Press.** Taken together, the works in the first part of this chapter construct a world much more global than contemporary readers might imagine; two works exploring these political systems are **Janet L. Abu-Lughod (1989).** *Before European Hegemony: The World System A. D. 1250–1350.* **Oxford: Oxford University Press** and **Parag Khanna (2011).** *How to Run the World: Charting a Course to the Next Renaissance.* **New York: Random House,** which looks back to the Middle Ages as the first truly global economy. Although primarily about romance, **Geraldine Heng (2003).** *Empire of Magic: Medieval Romance and the Politics of Cultural Fantasy.* **New York: Columbia University Press** examines the fantasies created by medieval literature, many of which touch on history, travel, and the imagined, exotic world of the "other." Readers more engaged by pilgrimage will find that **Donald R. Howard (1980).** *Writers and Pilgrims: Medieval Pilgrimage Narratives and their Posterity.* **Berkeley, CA: University of California Press, and available online:**https://books.google. com/books?id=oF3QD4b4GOEC&printsec=frontcover&source= gbs_ge_summary_r&cad=0#v=onepage&q&f=false focuses specifically on the literature of pilgrimage, while **Dianna Webb (2002).** *Medieval European Pilgrimage c.700–c. 1500.* **London: Palgrave** provides an historical overview of pilgrims, their routes, and their experiences throughout the medieval period.

6

THE MOST EXTREME
ICONIC AUTHORS OF THE
MIDDLE AGES

When Chaucer sends off his "litel bok," at the end of *Troilus and Criseyde*, his romance/epic version of the Trojan War story, a loose translation of Giovanni Boccaccio's *Filostrato*, he wishes that it will "subit be to alle poesye; / And kis the steppes where as thow seest pace / Virgile, Ovide, Omer, Lucan, Stace" (Chaucer 1987: V 1790–2) [subject be to all poetry / and kiss the steps where you have seen pass / Virgil, Ovid, Homer, Lucan, Statius]. Little did Chaucer imagine that he would be among the set of medieval writers whose steps future generations might seek to have their works kiss. He might also have been surprised to find himself in company with Dante and Boccaccio whose works had such significant influence on his own. Dante walks with Virgil and Statius through the *Inferno* and *Purgatorio*, paying them homage as his guides literal (at least within the narrative) and literary, and sees Ovid and Homer with the virtuous Pagans in Limbo. Boccaccio lectures on Dante, cementing his reputation, while Christine de Pizan responds to Boccaccio's *Concerning Famous Women* in her *Book of the City of Ladies*. Sir Thomas Malory and the author of *Sir Gawain and the Green Knight* both respond to the long history of Arthurian material, creating their own takes on a long-standing medieval tradition nearing its end. While they might be joined by many others – Augustine of Hippo, Hildegarde of Bingen, Chrétien de Troyes, Marie de France, the authors of *Beowulf*, the *Niebelungenlied*, or the *Chanson de Roland*, Snorri Sturluson, Jean de Meun, the list goes on – these writers have achieved a place in the canon as the literary representatives of the Middle Ages. Of course, their reputations vary from place to place; Boccaccio gets more attention than Chaucer in Italy, while Malory is likely read rarely in France because that country has its own robust Arthurian tradition, but these authors' names are certainly among the first thought of when medieval or "Great Books" syllabi get put together, or when one thinks of medieval literature.

We have spent most of this volume considering the different genres of medieval literature, and while these categories underlie much of the medieval literature read and studied in classrooms, there are several authors who resist confinement in any specific generic category. Many of them have written works that fall into one or more of the genres covered in other chapters – or, their influence and importance are great enough to warrant more specialized attention – and so we have decided to commit a chapter to these writers' works, talents, biographies, and continued influence in the present day. These, of course, are the "big names" of medieval literature – Dante Alighieri, Giovanni Boccaccio, Geoffrey Chaucer, Christine de Pizan, Thomas Malory, and the *Gawain-* or *Pearl*-poet. While we have generally tried to eschew exceptionalism through our choice of focus, these authors are exceptional because of their abilities to acquire – and in the case of Dante and Chaucer, maintain – their status for such an extended period of time and the ways that their works have been shown to be open to multiple approaches and examinations since their own time. While some of these authors fell out of favor between their own time and more recent years, such as Christine de Pizan, whose revival coincided with an interest in literature by women and the rise of feminist theory in the 1980s, and others have become far more famous in the contemporary world than they seem to have been in their own, such as the *Gawain*-poet, Chaucer and Dante received their "major author" status in their own time and have maintained their popularity (with some breaks) ever since. Boccaccio, famous in his own right, was also instrumental in building Dante's reputation and iconic status, while also providing significant fodder for Chaucer's work (even if Chaucer never acknowledges him directly). Malory, whose work is perhaps the least read in its original form, and who was hardly the first to make King Arthur a topic, spawned an entire industry of Arthurian material that continues to grow.

One of the many reasons these authors retain their importance and popularity today is their complexity. Medieval literature in general offers a great deal of complexity – as we hope we have shown throughout the volume – but these authors in particular present their readers with a series of ambiguities, problems, and challenges that make for very engaging – and sometimes troubling – reading. Chaucer is often noted for his ambiguity, and Dante is deeply engaged in knotty theological and allegorical readings, as well as political challenges; Christine de Pizan is notable for her participation in the *querelle-des-fames*, or debate about women, and Boccaccio is famously slippery. The *Gawain*-poet is particularly famous for his games, especially those that lie at the heart of *Sir Gawain and the Green Knight*. It is in this ludic spirit that we approach this chapter and invite readers to participate as well: after reading this far, and using your own knowledge about the Middle Ages and its authors, join the game and rate these authors using your own criteria. Would you use the same categories? Would you assess a different score for a particular author? Would you include any different authors? Do you agree with our final evaluation? Play along, and see which medieval author emerges, for you, as *the Most Extreme*.

BACKGROUND

In 2002, the television network Animal Planet released a series titled *The Most Extreme*. In each episode, the show focuses on a particular animal trait such as speed, survivability, strength, smarts, disguise, venom – or even more unique traits like piratical tendencies, gourmet food preparation, aptitude for playing dead, and psychic predisposition. The show then ranks ten animals based on how well they exhibit and have adapted that specific trait. In this chapter, our goal will be to conduct a similar experiment with some of the most iconic authors of the Middle Ages: versatile writers who have defied attempts at classification for centuries and thus have received a chapter all of their own.

Our approach will be slightly different than Animal Planet's in so far as our focus will be on a group of authors rather than a single authorial trait, and our evaluation will consist of how well those writers demonstrate a variety of writing talents. Those talents will include: **diversity** of work produced and versatility of the author (including major topics and themes of works and familiarity with various genres such as the epic, lyric, and fabliaux; whether he or she has written prose, poetry, and/or drama, and how familiar he or she was with languages other than a native tongue); **volume** of known works; **popularity** (although the popularity of some of these authors in their own time is clear by the number of manuscripts of their work or the many references to them by their contemporaries and near -descendants, others are harder to assess. There is only one extant manuscript of the *Gawain*-poet's and Malory's works, but both authors have acquired significant reputations since. Therefore, we are considering their popularity with their contemporary audience, including the geographical regions to which such author's works spread; and popularity today, including the extent of adaptations produced in present-day media, and reputation among students and the general public); amount of **scholarship** produced, focusing on the author or his or her works; and **accessibility** – can their works be taught in high school courses as well as universities, or enjoyed by the general reader?

Taking into consideration all of these factors, the conclusion of this chapter will reveal which famous medieval author is... *the Most Extreme*. While we attempt to provide as much background as possible for each author, it is impossible to cover every relevant detail in the space available. Some authors such as Dante and Chaucer have entire encyclopedias dedicated to their lives and works, and every author in this chapter has a large body of criticism written about their works, although for each of them, certain works stand out as their most popular, in part because they're the most commonly taught, whether they were the most popular at the time they were written or not, to the extent that medieval popularity can be determined. As in each of the previous chapters, we will provide suggestions for further reading, if a particular author is of special interest.

DANTE ALIGHIERI

Called by Poets.org a "masterwork of world literature," Dante Alighieri (born Durante degli Alighieri in Florence, Italy 1265) is most renowned for writing *La Divina Commedia* (circa 1308–21), or *The Divine Comedy*, originally called *Commedia* by its author, *Divina* being later added by Boccaccio. The poet dabbled in many subjects in his early years, including Tuscan poetry, painting, and music, in addition to the classical Latin poetry of Homer and Virgil. As part of his education in Florence as a member of a higher social class, he received instruction in Latin and engaged with members of Florence's literary circle, emulating a community of poets known as the Sicilian School and immersing himself in troubadour verse full of courtly love and the elevation of women. During this time, Dante associated with a local group of writers and philosophers who practiced the "*dolce stil nuovo* (or *novo*), the 'sweet new style' or just 'new style,' whose Tuscan members were called *stilnovisti*" (Hunt 2011: 21). The movement focused on writing in the vernacular and idealizing love and womanhood, influenced by the tradition of courtly love found in troubadour poetry and the philosophical doctrines of Thomism, Platonism, and Aristotelianism.

Dante's political involvement brought him away from his academic studies in 1289 when he fought (likely as a cavalry officer) at the battle of Campaldino in the Guelph-Ghibeline conflict, a division between those loyal to the Holy Roman Emperor and the Papacy. The Guelphs (loyal to the Pope) won the battle, but subsequently divided into two factions, the Whites (Dante's party) and the Blacks. The Blacks took control of the city, and Dante was eventually exiled in 1302. In 1293–4, Dante penned his first major work known as the *Vita Nuova*, described as "a poetic anthology filled with his musing about love, especially its spiritual dimensions" (Hunt 2011: 23).

Circa 1308, Dante began work on *La Commedia*, a partly auto-biographical work that departed from the tradition of epic national histories found in Homer and Virgil. The text is strongly motivated by the political strife and violence permeating Florence during Dante's time as the poet considered the conflict between papacy and aristocracy, corruption and morality, nobility and mediocracy. Dante belonged to the political party that advocated for a greater independence from Rome, and this philosophy emerges throughout *The Divine Comedy* as characters based on historical popes (or named outright as specific popes) are found suffering punishments for their sins in *Inferno*, either trapped in a whirlwind at the gates of hell, or embedded upside down in mud with flames burning their feet.

He never again returned to Florence, despite a conditional offer of amnesty in 1315, staunchly refusing to admit any prior guilt against the city. He published *Purgatorio* at this time, after publishing the *Inferno* the year prior. In 1321, he completed *Paradiso* and died shortly afterwards on September 13, 1321 in Ravenna. Florence later attempted to have his remains transferred back to the city, even building an empty monument-tomb in his honor in the basilica of Santa Croce. Although he did not receive any formal distinction as a poet laureate during his life, he is often depicted in famous posthumous portraits as wearing a laurel crown. According to Peter Hawkins, he was well versed in poetry, prose, literary history and theory, philosophy, and political science; he also "wears many hats: he is poet, memoirist, and literary critic of his own efforts" (2006: 7). Dante wrote letters to contemporaries, including correspondences addressed to bishops, counts, senators, princes, cardinals, and even King Henry VII of England; a political treatise (*De Monarchia*, circa 1308–18); critical/scholarly pieces (*Convivio*, circa 1304–7); one piece (*La Vita Nuova,* 1295) that combines several styles, described as "a fusion of secular lyric tradition with the conventions and interests of scholastic philosophy… [W]hile the narrative line is simple enough, the implications of allegory, the carefully planned ambiguities, and some quite strategic reticences open the way to a great variety of interpretations" (Bergin 1965: 67); and religious and social satire, exemplified most notably by *La Divina Commedia*, which is itself described as being "part narrative, part descriptive, part dramatic, part epic, part exhortatory, part satiric and part lyric" (Reynolds 2006: 116).

La Divina Commedia is viewed by many as Dante's most revolutionary work. It exhibits innovation in style and structure, creating the *terza rima* form (ABA, BCB, CDC), and demonstrating a variety of distinct voices within the narrative. There are even forays into Latin, Greek, Hebrew, and Provençal within the text, giving Dante a breadth unmatched by many of his successors. It is divided into three *cantiche* (*Inferno, Purgatorio*, and *Paradiso*), each consisting of thirty-three cantos (chapters) plus one introductory canto, bringing the total number to one hundred. Barbara Reynolds claims that:

The concluding cantos of *Paradiso* represent Dante's literary skills brought to their highest pitch: variety of narrative, compelling dialogue, surprise, ethereal pictorial similes, rich and colourful imagery, visions of the universe, together with startling contrasts in style, changing suddenly from the sublime to invective.

(Reynolds 2006: 372).

Among Dante's contemporaries, "The *Commedia* was an immediate hit, and not only among the 7 percent of the total population who were the *literati*" (Hawkins 2006: 24). It was written primarily in vernacular Italian, and so was intended for the masses (despite Dante's original attempt to write the piece in Latin, which was the language of choice for authors in that time period). Ultimately, it became an attempt on Dante's part to connect with the people, and it worked, sometimes to the dismay of the more educated. Because the epic genre was commonly written in Latin or Greek (with Virgil and Homer setting the foundation for such a style), some such as Giovanni del Vergilio, a correspondent of Dante's, believed that the *Commedia's* audience should have been limited to Latinists who were sufficiently educated to understand the allusions, allegories, and references, overt or subtle as they might be.

The laypeople who engaged with the *Commedia*, on the other hand, cried out for public readings of the text, and Giovanni Boccaccio "began a cycle of performance and exegesis of the poem at the church of San Stefano di Badia. Although he covered only about half of the *Inferno*, his effort became an institution" (Hawkins 2006: 26). Boccaccio himself drew inspiration from Dante's work, not only writing in praise of the poet but writing texts such as *Il Corbaccio* that parallel the structure of the *Commedia* as well. According to Hawkins, "Many of the stories in [Boccaccio's] renowned vernacular collection, the *Decameron*, owed their origins to characters and episodes that first appeared in the *Commedia*" (2006: 26).

Even to this day, there are still groups dedicated to performing and interpreting Dante's work, carrying on Boccacio's tradition. Hawkins writes: "according to the website of San Francisco's venerable Shrine Church of Saint Francis…'The *Lectura Dantis* group meets Wednesday evenings at 7:30 PM in the basement of the church for informal discussion'" (2006: 27). In addition to informal reading, Dante has become a staple in high school and college English and literature courses, not to mention the numerous adaptations of his work, including Larry Niven and Jerry Pournelle's novel *Inferno* (1976), Dan Brown's novel *Inferno* (2013 – author of *The Da Vinci Code* and *Angels & Demons*), several film productions (of both Dante's work as well as the literary adaptations of it), and even a video game produced by EA Games in 2010. It is probably safe to assume that most college students and high school graduates in the United States and Europe have heard of Dante Alighieri, *The Inferno*, or *The Divine Comedy*.

As an extremely diverse and influential writer of the Middle Ages (though perhaps not quite so prolific), Dante scores highly in categories such as diversity and popularity, and less so in those like volume. His ratings (out of ten) are:

Diversity: 9; Volume: 6; Popularity: 10; Scholarship: 9; Accessibility: 9

GIOVANNI BOCCACCIO

The successor of Dante in medieval Italian literature, Giovanni Boccaccio was born in 1313 in Tuscany, Italy, to a wealthy merchant father and an unknown mother. Boccaccino di Chellino, Boccaccio's father, eventually married Margherita de' Mardoli whose family was ancestrally related to Dante's biographical Beatrice. Thus, Giovanni Boccaccio could boast of a distant relation to the poet he so admired. In 1330, Boccaccio took up the study of canon law before moving to Paris in 1332 where he pursued his humanist interests in literature, documented by some of his early essays written in Latin and his first vernacular poetry. Here, his encyclopedic interests were cultivated; having been admitted to a learned circle that regularly met at the Royal Library, Boccaccio had access to classical Latin literature such as Ovid and Virgil; Provençal and Old French Romances; and scholarly compilations discussing mythology, astrology, history, and even magic and alchemy. Thus, Boccaccio's twofold culture emerged: poetic, in a progressive, humanistic sense, and encyclopedic in a medieval sense.

As such, Boccaccio became an extremely diverse author. His works include letters written in Latin, intellectual essays, vernacular poetry, lyric poetry, romance (combined with epic romance), genealogies and encyclopedic texts, biography, frame narratives, elegy, social satire, critical and scholarly tractates, humanistic ethnography, and allegorical eclogues. Like Dante, Boccaccio also at times added autobiographical flourishes to his work, particularly in his *Filocolo* (1335–6) – a five-book volume that recounts for the first time in Italian prose the Byzantine legend of Florio, son of the King of Marmorina, and Biancifiore, a poor girl with unknown, princely Roman origins – and *Il Corbaccio* (c. 1350s or 1360s), a satire that describes a narrator who suffers from an ill-fated love affair and is remarkably parallel to Dante's *Divina Commedia*. Scholars and critics have long pondered how autobiographical this work truly is, with no definitive answer on the subject. Whether memoir or pseudo-autobiographical fiction, *Il Corbaccio* remains for some a paradigm of Boccaccio's work, exhibiting his diversity as a writer and his ability to create a text that ranges from "a reported autobiographical account at one end, through an imagined realistic experience in the middle, and a self-aware manipulation of literary forms at the other" (Brown University Italian Studies Department 2014).

Boccaccio also manipulated various forms and genres within a single text. The *Decameron* (circa 1348–53), perhaps his most well-known work, is a frame narrative in which themes of social, aristocratic, and bourgeoisie lifestyle emerge alongside the impacts of plague-stricken Europe, considerations of humankind striving against fate and learning to overcome it, religious commentary, and a balance of solemnity and joviality. There is also a symmetry between erudite ornamentation and a layman's narrative, making the text of critical interest for contemporary scholars and a literary pleasure for the masses.

Following in Dante's footsteps, Boccaccio worked not only in the classical forms and the Latin language, but also the vernacular, making his work accessible to the laypeople as well as the scholars. According to Umberto Bosco:

> In the broad sweep of its range and its alternately tragic and comic views of life, [the *Decameron*] is rightly regarded as [Boccaccio's] masterpiece. Stylistically, it is the most perfect example of Italian classical prose, *and its influence on Renaissance literature throughout Europe was enormous.*
>
> (2014, emphasis added)

Additionally, the nineteenth-century critic Francesco De Sanctis is known for viewing the *Decameron* as a successor to Dante's *Commedia*, calling it a "Human Comedy" and dubbing Boccaccio a pioneer of a new moral order that would supersede that of the European Middle Ages. In humanist and Renaissance studies taking place during Boccaccio's time, he was often viewed as one who turned his attention and the attentions of others to not only the Greek and Latin classics but also to more contemporary Italian literature, especially that of Dante, his immediate predecessor. However, despite his later critical acclamation, Boccaccio – like Dante – faced contemporary criticism from erudite society.

Giuseppe Mazzotta explains that, "From the time when just a few of its stories were circulating… the *Decameron* has been viewed as something of a scandal in the canon of Italian and European letters" and that it faced a "patronizing reception… by the more conspicuous intellectuals of Italian Humanism" (1986: 3). Storytelling that did not conform to scholarly standards became "domestic trifles" and the scholars of the time "never hid either their preference for Boccaccio the humanist or their astonishment at his encyclopedic erudition that would find its way into works such as the *Geneology of the Gentile Gods*" (Mazzotta 1986: 3).

Boccaccio, then, negotiated the realms of academia and imagination and faced criticism in doing so. His own opinions about the *Decameron* itself, never entirely clear, fluctuate between a "passionate defense of the novella… to his narrative posture that the stories are nothing more than innocuous pieces of entertainment for ladies, to the equally passionate rejection, in [a] letter to Mainardo Cavalcanti, of the book's dangerous morality" (Mazzotta 1986: 4). Whether a decadent trifle, a "mimesis of reality" that mirrors rising mercantile interests, a "militant polemic in favor of Naturalism," or an "esthetic escape into a pleasant landscape" (Mazzotta 1986: 5), the *Decameron* has certainly endured throughout history as a work that demonstrates Boccaccio's "awareness of the distance separating facts from values, the recognition of the instability of our common assumptions, as well as of the crisis investing moral and intellectual systems" (Mazzotta 1986: 6–7). The work, as Mazzotta claims:

> without ever leaving the world of reality and, actually, by sinking into it more deeply than has been acknowledged, launches us into the realm

of the imagination where we confront the traps of delusion characters construct for others and, consequently, for themselves.

(Mazzotta 1986: 7)

Although the *Decameron* is certainly Boccaccio's most well-known work, some others include *Il Filostrato* (c. 1338), which would become the inspiration for Geoffrey Chaucer's *Troilus and Criseyde* and William Shakespeare's play of the same title; *Teseida* (c. 1340–1), which would offer Chaucer the background for his *Knight's Tale; De Genealogia Deorum Gentilium* (On the Genealogy of the Gods of the Gentiles, likely begun in 1350 and continuously corrected and revised until his death); *De Claris Mulieribus* (On Famous Women, 1360–74); *Tratatello in Laude di Dante* (Tractate in Praise of Dante, 1357–61); and *Buccolicum Carmen* (a composition of short pastoral poems, 1351–66).

In 1373, Boccaccio was also officially commissioned by the Guild Priors and Gonfalonier of Justice of the People and Commune of Florence to give public lectures on Dante's *Divine Comedy*, in part elevating Dante to the popularity for which he is known today. Boccaccio's *Expositions*, as Michael Papio describes, "have for centuries been considered the best of the early commentaries on Dante's masterpiece" (2009: 3). In them, Boccaccio artfully illustrates and emphasizes Dante's literary prowess, considers the ways in which poetry can "transmit immutable truths about human nature" (Papio 2009: 4), and praises Dante's use of new poetic forms to do just that. Additionally, his *Expositions* serve as explanations or glosses of denser passages within the *Comedy*, though Boccaccio himself was rather critical of his own work. In a later letter to an unidentified acquaintance, Boccaccio "ruefully acknowledges and accepts the blame for having peeled back the poetic veil of Dante's *Comedy* so that its meaning could be understood by venal merchants and the common man" (Papio 2009: 6). Nevertheless, they influenced later commentators on Dante's work, and "neither its moments of narrative flair nor its consistent efforts to underscore Dante's genius… are sufficient to explain the real historical importance of such a consequential literary and cultural contribution" (Papio 2009: 3).

While Boccaccio might not be as popular as Dante in academia or popular culture, Katherine Adams Brown considers the ways in which Boccaccio evokes the question of readership in his frame narrative that "bridges the gap between writer and reader, producer and consumer, text and imagination" (Katherine Brown 2014: 163), establishing a relationship between literature and people that would continue through the Middle Ages even to the present day. Mazzotta further argues that:

> each chapter [in the *Decameron*] retrieves a particular intellectual tradition... – medical texts, for instance, and Boccaccio's sense of the crisis of scientific discourse, the vocabulary and values of courtly love, legal lore, etc. – in order to define the cultural frame of reference for the narrative... [F]or Boccaccio, literature and the resources of imagination and desire, which are the matter of literature, shape every experience in the *Decameron*.
>
> (Mazzotta 1986: xv)

Like Dante, Boccaccio explores the realms of possibility through intellectual writings and through storytelling, sometimes combining the two modes, often engaging with morality and humanism to earn his place as a medieval icon.

Boccaccio's influence in the Middle Ages and on other authors, both contemporary and future, marks him as an iconic medieval writer who explored human nature in a variety of genres and forms. And while scholarship on Boccaccio might be more limited, he enjoys his own "American Boccaccio Association" founded in 1974 that promotes the study and teaching of Boccaccio's life and works. His scores are:

Diversity: 9; Volume: 7; Popularity: 5; Scholarship: 6; Accessibility: 5

THE *GAWAIN*-POET

The anonymous writer dubbed by scholars as the *Gawain*-poet is attributed with the authorship of four, or possibly five, works: *Sir Gawain and the Green Knight*, *Pearl*, *Cleanness* (or *Purity*), and *Patience*, which make up the *Gawain Manuscript* (the richly illustrated British Library Cotton Nero A.x), and *Saint Erkenwald* (1386), which is sometimes attributed to the same author. The works of the *Gawain Manuscript* form a collection of moral tales that, if penned by the same poet, mark him or her as one of the three greatest English writers of the late Middle Ages. Yet, no firm evidence has, as of now, been discovered to concretely attribute these four works to the same author. Circumstantial evidence strongly suggests it, the most convincing of which being the manuscript in which these four narratives are found. Additionally, none of these works appears in any other surviving manuscript. Stylistic similarities, as well as dialect and vocabulary consistencies, point to a single author writing all four. Morphology and inflections used in the language of the narratives, as well as terms used to describe objects, artifacts, and clothing, indicate that the poems were likely written between 1350 and 1400.

Much scholarship has been devoted to discovering the identity of the *Gawain*-poet, and whether a single author did indeed pen all four works. Some studies look at internal cryptographic evidence within the poems and suggest that the identity of the poet was John Massey, though this is nothing more than speculation. The *Gawain*-poet participated in the Alliterative Revival, bringing back the traditional poetic forms from Old English poetry, whose forms included alliteration, specific patterns of stress, and caesuras, or regular internal line breaks. The *Gawain*-poet was somewhat free with this style, adding to the end of each alliterative stanza a five-line, rhymed section called the "bob and wheel" – a very short, two-word line (the bob) followed by four short rhymed lines (the wheel) to *Sir Gawain and the Green Knight*. The other three poems are in more traditional alliterative style, although *Pearl* is broken into stanzas and sections.

In terms of diversity and volume, this chapter will cede to the majority of scholarship which assigns all four works to a single author. Even so, the four narratives themselves have similar structures and concerns, dealing with the trials of human life and often serving as moral lessons for readers. *Patience* and *Cleanness* are both narrative homilies, the first of which looks at the Sermon on the Mount as described in the Gospel of St. Matthew and the virtues it preaches, particularly patience, which it then exemplifies through counter-example of the Biblical story of Jonah, who embodies impatience in his inability to accept his divine duty to preach to the Ninevites. Because God still shows mercy to Jonah, the poem also emphasizes God's love for all his creatures, even those who do not fulfill ideal virtues. *Cleanness*, as its title suggests, focuses on the joys of purity and the dangers of defilement. The poem tells the parable of the wedding feast found in the Gospels of Matthew and Luke to illustrate the joys of married love, while the tales of Sodom and Gemorrah and the fall of Belshazzer, who defiles the Temple vessels during the Babylonian Captivity, serve as examples of the dangers of defilement.

Pearl, which consists of 101 twelve-line stanzas in iambic tetrameter, is a dream-vision allegory and, if read as autobiographical in nature, an elegy because the young girl spoken of in the poem is sometimes thought to be the poet's daughter. In it, the dreamer falls asleep and sees a vision of the Pearl Maiden standing on the opposite bank of a river; he then asks if she is the Pearl he has lost. She offers a theological answer, saying that the pearl he refers to was a rose that withered; she then offers him a vision of the Heavenly City and shows herself to be part of the retinue of Christ, figured as the Lamb. In his desire to join her, the dreamer falls into the river and awakens, meditating on theological virtue and promising to fulfill the will of God so that he can join the Pearl Maiden. The dream-vision genre invites fictionality, though, and there is no way of knowing for certain whether the poem's speaker is indeed speaking with the poet's voice. The poet creates challenges through his narrative voice; the dreamer (speaker) of the poem has a somewhat obtuse nature, which contrasts so strongly with the theological sophistication of the poet's ideology, making it difficult to conflate them into a single figure. This creates one of the poet's particular forms of contradiction, since the poet could not have been authentically ignorant and yet knowledgeable enough to illustrate the doctrinal message which the Pearl Maiden preaches.

Less overtly doctrinal than the three poems it accompanies, *Sir Gawain and the Green Knight*, believed by some to be the most perfectly structured poem of all Middle English romances, is above all else a narrative concerned with chivalry – the way ideal medieval knighthood should operate. It is idealistic in its considerations, as chivalry itself is an ideal system and thus not one achieved in reality. Sir Gawain, the most perfect of knights, according to the poet, is tested throughout the poem in his ability to remain virtuous and to uphold his promises. Challenged to a beheading game by the magical Green Knight, Gawain first thinks he has won because he cuts off the Green Knight's head; however, the Green Knight picks up his head, which calls to Gawain to keep his part of the promise as the Knight rides out of Arthur's Hall. The greatest test comes when Gawain must remain pure against the attempted seductions of Bertilak's wife. To betray his benefactor by sleeping with his wife would be disastrous, and, as the perfect knight, Gawain remains pure, though not without committing a small transgression for which he must later confess, namely his with-holding of a girdle despite his promise to give to Bertilak each day whatever his spoils might be.

Sir Gawain and the Green Knight is a poem filled with games, contests, exchanges, and knots; indeed, the pentangle, or endless knot, on Gawain's shield may be taken as a kind of metaphor for the poem, as can the green girdle which Lady Bertilak gives to Gawain on the third night. In the *Poem as Green Girdle*, R. A. Shoaf comments that "the poem's emphasis on signs and tokens... is an integral part of its larger concern with order and meaning in civilization" (Shoaf 1984: 4). The pentangle, representing the five wounds of Christ, the five fingers, five wits, five sorrows of Mary, and ultimately the five chivalric virtues; and the girdle, representing (in Shoaf's analysis) commercial exchange, and in other readings both Gawain's failure and his success, create a series of complexities in determining the poem's meaning. Both symbols offer the reader opportunities for multiple readings which often conflict with each other, making the poem itself a complex knot.

With only one surviving manuscript that contains these works, medieval popularity may not have been anywhere near as wide-spread as authors such as Chaucer or Dante, and the poem's Northern dialect makes it more challenging reading for con-temporary students than Chaucer's Midland dialect, which formed the basis of Modern English.

Despite the division of *Sir Gawain and the Green Knight* into four sections, which suggests that the poem might have been originally meant to be read aloud, the poet's esoteric vocabulary would necessarily have restricted it to an audience who shared the poet's dialect. Additionally, rare words are used in arcane senses, further limiting who might have read or listened to this work. That said, many authors, such as J. R. R. Tolkien, John Gardner, W. S. Merwin, and Simon Armitage, have found *Sir Gawain and the*

Green Knight compelling and have produced lively translations. These, and several scholarly editions emphasizing both accuracy and the poem's alliterative style, have made the poem accessible to modern audiences.

Early scholarship dedicated to the *Gawain*-poet focuses not only on the works but also, as mentioned earlier, on the controversy surrounding the identity of the poet and whether or not all four works found in the Cotton Nero A.x manuscript can be accurately attributed to one person. More contemporary readings have found the poem rich fodder to study medieval engagement with land and the environment, sexuality, desire, emotion, monstrosity, and alterity, and these have joined studies of the poem's use of gender, symbolism, language, and history. Although the poem has not accrued the number of adaptations that other Arthurian romances have, elements of it appear in novels, television shows, and, notably two feature films, *Sir Gawain and the Green Knight* (1973) and *Sword of the Valiant* (1984), featuring Sean Connery as the Green Knight. Oddly, both films were made by the same director, and while both resemble the poem at their start and finish, they depart wildly from it in the middle. The poem has been made into three different operas and several plays.

The other texts in Cotton Nero A.x have not received the same attention, nor has *St. Erkenwald*. While there is a handful of scholarship on *Cleanness, Patience,* and *St. Erkenwald, Pearl* has received the most scholarly attention after *Sir Gawain and the Green Knight*, and none of the other poems have received the same range of criticism and depth of inquiry. They have thus far not been adapted for a modern audience, although there are several translations available for those who wish to explore these under-represented works. If they do not offer *Sir Gawain and the Green Knight's* excitement, they nevertheless remain some of the English Middle Ages' most beautiful poetry.

Diversity: 3; Volume: 3; Popularity: 6; Scholarship: 3; Accessibility: 5

GEOFFREY CHAUCER

The first major author to write works in the English language, Geoffrey Chaucer was born circa 1343 in London, England, and enjoyed a varied life and career, including public service as an esquire to the king and a diplomat who served missions in Florence and Genoa, among other foreign locales. His work as an author and poet began around 1369, with the *Book of the Duchess* and an *ABC* poem, both lyrics written in English, which may, for a modern reader, not be such a curious phenomenon. However, as Jeffrey Helterman explains:

> The first impulse for a medieval writer who was writing something he wanted remembered was to write it in Latin. Latin was considered to be the *grammatic*, the language which would not change, the indestructible language.
>
> (Helterman 1994: 128)

Chaucer, then, follows the impulse of Dante and Boccaccio in writing not only in a language other than Latin, but in English, the language considered the most common in England after the Norman Conquest in 1066 when the French took control of the aristocracy. And Chaucer certainly was fluent in both French and Latin, marrying into a French aristocratic family through his union with Phillipa, the sister-in-law of John of Gaunt, the most powerful man in England at the time – more powerful, even, than the king himself.

Following his early work, Chaucer continued to write dream visions such as *The House of Fame* (1378–81), *Parliament of Fowles* (1378–81), *Complaint of Venus* (c. 1380–6), and *Complaint of Mars* (c. 1380–6). Longer romances such as *Troilus and Criseyde* (1382–6), which "analyzes the artifices of love as well as the complex motivations of lovers" (Helterman 1994: 135), and *Anelida and Arcite* (c. late 1370s) draw their inspiration from Italian writers such as Dante and Boccacio, whose works Chaucer likely encountered during his trips to Italy in the 1370s. Some claim that *Troilus and Criseyde* is the first English novel, "based on the way Chaucer handled the psychology of the main characters. They are always operating at two levels of response, verbal and intellectual" (Helterman 1994: 135). In *The Legend of Good Women* (c. 1386), "Chaucer castigates himself for doing a disservice to love by publishing the unfaithfulness of women, [and so the poet figure] responds to this charge from the god of love by telling stories of faithful women, love's martyrs" (Helterman 1994: 136).

Love, both courtly and basic, becomes an important theme with which Chaucer grapples, particularly in his greatest known work, *The Canterbury Tales* (1387–1400), an unfinished collection of frame narratives (like the *Decameron*, though Helterman claims it is "a brilliant advance on the [genre] as practiced by Boccaccio" [1994: 137]). According to George Lyman Kittredge, "most of the tales… center on discussions of marriage" though Helterman counters that by suggesting "what may be occurring in the frame tale of Canterbury storytelling is the social-climbers' revenge" (Helterman 1994: 137), balancing "high-class" tales with those like the Miller's, which offers, "among other things, a lower-class parody of the plot outlined in the Knight's Tale (two apparently similar men fight over the same woman) [and] becomes the first tale motivated by answering the previous tale" (Helterman 1994: 137). Animosity between social classes and the subtle distinctions between them become the focus of much of *The Canterbury Tales*, in addition to themes about marriage, authorship, and the act of reading and writing. He suggests in the Nun's Priest's Tale that the reader must "Taketh the fruyt, and lat the chaf be stille" [Take the fruit and leave the chaff (or waste)], apparently divesting himself of responsibility for how a reader might interpret the morality of the tale or indeed how an audience would read it.

While many of the tales are in direct dialogue with one another, either answering, continuing, or parodying another told before it, there are some tales within the text that end mid-sentence, or begin without any distinct motivation. Additionally, from information in the General Prologue, there are not nearly enough stories in the collection to fulfill the promise of four stories from each pilgrim, which would total 120 tales in all. There are also contentions among scholars as to the order of the tales (aside from the fixed tales which comprise the beginning), with the most common order based on the *Ellesmere Manuscript* (which dates between 1400 and 1405, and is currently housed at the Huntington Library in California, USA). Chaucer himself offers a reason in his "Retraction" for not finishing the work, claiming that the work was impious and sinful, though scholars debate the authenticity of such a "deathbed confession" and wonder if it appears simply as a medieval convention where "the apologetic voice allows Chaucer to list all his works while taking on the persona of the humble author, a stance favored in the Middle Ages" (Helterman 1994: 142).

Despite his inability to finish the work, Chaucer covers a vast breadth of literary forms and genres in *The Canterbury Tales* alone, making him, perhaps, one of the most diverse authors of the Middle Ages. Within the text, readers can find the *exemplum*, a brief and pointed tale told to illustrate a moral point; the Breton *lai*, a short romance often involving love and the supernatural (an example of which would be the Franklin's Tale, which is itself adapted from Boccaccio's *Il Filocolo*); the religious fable, found in the Clerk's Tale (which is also originally told in Boccaccio's *Decameron*, and then retold by Petrarch in Latin, which becomes the source for Chaucer's version); the Estates Satire, found in the General Prologue; the epic, found in the Knight's Tale; the romance, found in the Wife of Bath's Tale; the fabliau, a tale involving bawdy humor, found in the Miller's Tale; the hagiography, or tale of saints' lives, either real or fictionalized, found in the Man of Law's Tale; the sermon (didactic speeches often in prose) found in the Tale of Melibee; fables, found in the Nun's Priest's Tale, and Manciple's Tale; the tragedy, found in the Monk's Tale; satire, found in the Tale of Sir Thopas and the Squire's Tale; the alchemical tale, found in the Canon's Yeoman's Tale; the classical adaptation (such as Ovid's *Metamorphoses*, retold in the Manciple's Tale, or the Physician's Tale, which draws from the *Romance of the Rose*, even though Chaucer attributes his source to Titus Livius, a Roman historian); and the unfinished or interrupted tale, such as the Cook's Tale. (The tales listed as examples are not all-inclusive, and are meant as a quick reference-guide for interested readers.)

Aside from the various genres used by Chaucer in *The Canterbury Tales*, Chaucer also employs different forms of poetry and prose such as the couplet (which is the form used in most of the text, matching coupling lines with end rhymes); the rhyme royale, following the form ABABBCC, introduced and made popular in the English language by Chaucer himself; extended rhyme royale, found in the Monk's Tale; tail rhyme stanzas (Tale of Sir Thopas); and prose, found in the Tale of Melibee and the Parson's Tale. And as varied as the genres and forms are in the text, the characters are equally diverse, ranging from nobility to the merchant and working class to the clerical and religious.

Chaucer's popularity spread even during his own lifetime. By 1380, he was widely acclaimed for his poetry. His fame even reached France where the poet Eustache Deschamps praised Chaucer as a "great translator" and the "Ovid of the English tongue." Chaucer is additionally hailed as a "poet of love" by the English poet John Gower; as a philosopher by Chaucer's younger contemporary, Thomas Usk; and as a writer of eloquent style by fifteenth-century poets Thomas Hoccleve and John Lydgate. In contemporary culture, Chaucer's stories and tales, especially the fabliaux, find resonance, with reference to the Miller's Tale appearing in the television series *Big Bang Theory* (2010: S4, E8). Even rappers like Baba Brinkman have found Chaucer's poems easily translatable into a contemporary idiom.

Prolific and diverse, influential and innovative, Chaucer leaves a legacy that transcends the Middle Ages. Redefining authorship and the relationship between writer and reader, Chaucer employs an immense variety of methods and modes to interrogate society, religion, and humanity. He builds upon the foundations established by Dante and Boccaccio and adds his own terraces, verandas, and castles. His scores are:

Diversity: 10; Volume: 9; Popularity: 8; Scholarship: 9; Accessibility: 9

CHRISTINE DE PIZAN

All of what scholars know about the life of Christine de Pizan comes from references made within her own works, including her autobiographical *Lavision-Christine* (c. 1405). She is estimated to have been born between the years of 1364 and 1365 in Venice, Italy. Her father was Tommaso di Benvenuto da Pizzano, the court astrologer for Charles V, King of France. Christine soon joined her father in France where her education was fostered, exposing her to great scientific and philosophical literature as well as the Greek and Latin classics. Around the age of fifteen, Christine married a notary of the French court, Estienne de Castel, who supported her intellectual pursuits. Together they had three children before his death in 1390 (which is known from a statement she made mentioning her widowhood at the age of twenty-five when her husband died while accompanying the French King Charles VI to Beauvais).

The passing of her husband sparked the first of three stages that comprised her writing career: the literary.

Les Cent Balades, her first major work written between 1395 and 1400, uses individual poems to form a narrative and combines courtly form with worldly content, discussing issues such as the moral folly of individuals and the bleak reality of short-lived love affairs. This infusion of social portraits within courtly poetics heralds Christine's departure from the conventions of earlier poets. From her lyrical work, Christine began writing in allegory – the second stage – relying heavily on her historical knowledge and significant education to bolster the authenticity of her writings. In L'Epistre d'Othea [The Letter of Othea, c. 1400], Christine annotated one hundred illustrations of scenes from classical mythology, adding a verse text, a gloss, and an allegory, and between 1404 and 1405, Christine wrote Le Livre de la Cité des Dames [The Book of the City of Ladies], marking her as an early feminist writer. Her work shows a concern for the rights of women and the effects of clerical, courtly, and cultural misogyny.

The Livre de la Cité des Dames and its follow-up, the Tresor de la Cité des Dames, or the Livre au Trois Vertues (1405) [The Treasure of the City of Ladies; or The Book of the Three Virtues], grow out of Christine's engagement in the querelle des femmes, or "the woman question," a public debate in which she participated, defending women from misogynist attacks levied against them by the church and the state. She entered the querelle de la rose, a debate about the Roman de la Rose by Jean de Meun (see Chapter 3), rebutting Jean's anti-feminist romance which scorned courtly love, instead ridiculing love and desire which idealized women. Presenting her case to the Queen of France, Christine introduced women into public scholarly and political debate. Her entrance provided a public forum in which women could develop their literary talents.

The Cité des Dames and the Tresor de la Cité des Dames are both allegories in which the female figures of Reason, Rectitude, and Justice school Christine and her readers in the appropriate understanding of women in opposition to the misogynist literature of her time, particularly Matheolus' Lamentations (13th century). Picking up the work for some light reading at the start of the Cité des Dames, she finds herself appalled at the vision of women and becomes depressed, but is revived when the three allegorical ladies appear before her to set the record straight. They urge her to build a City of Ladies – an echo of Augustine's City of Man and City of God – with the building blocks consisting of all the important ladies from history and the inhabitants the Virgin Mary and the female saints. Christine's City consists of women from history, classical mythology (pagan goddesses appear as accomplished women inventors, fighters, and lovers), literature, and religion. In a sense, she revises Boccaccio's *De Claris Mulieribus* (1374), although the two texts share a sense that women should have more say in their own lives as well as access to education, which for Christine seems more formal and structured than it does for Boccaccio. She draws, as well, from the *Decameron*, from Petrarch, and other medieval writers.

In the three parts, she seeks to demonstrate women's inventions, accomplishments, virtues, and contributions. Women emerge as powerful rulers, inventors, educators, and leaders. In Christine's telling, figures often appear quite differently than they do in other works. For instance, Medea, generally considered to be a sorceress and a dark figure, appears in the *Cité* as:

> very beautiful, with a noble and upright heart and a pleasant face. In learning, however, she surpassed and exceeded all women; she knew the powers of every herb and all the potions which could be concocted, and she was ignorant of no art which can be known.
>
> (Christine 1982: 69)

Medea's revenge against Jason is reinterpreted – while Medea "loved Jason with a too great and too constant love" (Christine 1982: 189), he "lied about his promise, for after everything went just as he wanted, he left Medea for another woman. For this reason, Medea, who would rather have destroyed herself than do anything of this kind to him, turned despondent, nor did her heart ever again feel goodness or joy" (Christine 1982: 190). In revising the stories of famous women, Christine suggests that the story is as much a product of who tells it as the women it concerns; men's versions, she implies, will always misjudge and misunderstand women, turning their virtues into vices in order to cover up their own misbehavior. Therefore, the City of Ladies provides a safe space for women to tell their own stories. She writes the sequel for women's education; the *Tresor* also begins with Reason, Rectitude, and Justice urging her to action (in one of the miniatures in the manuscript, they are pulling her out of bed) so that she can educate women of all statuses and professions in wise conduct and behavior.

Readers often find the end of the *Cité* problematic, because Christine urges real women to put up with their husbands, good or bad, and attempt to reform them, while looking for rewards in the world to come. However, it remains useful to consider the context of the work and when it is written, as well as the somewhat transgressive nature of the *Tresor*, which offers an education to women from laundresses to queens before passing judgement on Christine's last page. It is not fair to condemn her for failing to put forward a contemporary feminist agenda when such a thing was inconceivable in 1405, and to do so is to miss the value of her work.

Growing out of her participation in the *Querelle* and her feminist writings, the third stage – her political writings – was concretized in 1405 when Christine composed a letter to the Queen of France in response to King Charles VI's descent into madness. The letter appeals to Isabeau to mediate between rival court factions fighting in the midst of intrigue, wars, and a political vacuum created by Charles' instability. In her *Epistre de la prison de vie humaine* [Letter on the Prison of Human Life, c. 1415–18], Christine consoles the survivors and widows of the Battle of Agincourt in which the French suffered defeat at the hands of the English. Her final work, *La Ditie de Jeanne d'Arc* [The Tale of Joan of Arc, 1429] celebrates the first military victories of Joan of Arc over the English. It is unclear whether Christine survived to know of Joan's capture and execution in 1431, as she (Christine) is referred to in the past tense by 1434 in a text of Guillebert de Mets, a member of the court of Burgandy. However, it is clear in the *Ditie* that Joan of Arc would earn a noble place in the City of Ladies.

Throughout her literary career, Christine shifted from a lyric poet and a master of courtly forms to a political writer pointedly concerned with the issues of peace and justice. She was well versed in complex metrical forms such as the ballad, lay, and rondeaux, and she integrated personal, political, moral, religious, and feminist themes within those narrative structures. Like Chaucer, she has a very diverse bibliography, with genres ranging from poetry to prose to epistles and biographies (in 1403, Phillip of Burgandy commissioned Christine to write a biography of his father, King Charles V) – and a versatility of themes appear throughout her work.

Although her works were among the first printed books in France and England, Christine received a limited reception throughout Western Europe until the twentieth century. Still, she is considered to be an innovative writer in the French language, coining words still used in the present day. Her Latinate syntax combined with the vernacular demonstrated her elevated education. Scenes from her *Cité des Dames* appear in fifteenth-century tapestries for noblewomen in Burgundy, speaking to the popularity of her writing and the prevalence of her social concerns. Even in the nineteenth-century women's rights movements, Christine was recognized as an early feminist who wasn't afraid to speak about concerns regarding the mistreatment of women and the misogyny of the patriarchy.

When the first Modern English translation of *Cites des Dames* was published in 1982, scholarly interest in Christine de Pizan's works rekindled outside of France. In her biography of Christine, Charity Cannon Willard observes: "In reading the works that Christine left behind her, one is struck repeatedly by her intense desire to be remembered by posterity" (Willard 1984: 211). Although she has always been known in France, it was not until the 1980s that she truly regained the reputation she enjoyed in her own time. Because of the content of her work, there have been modern translations but no modern adaptations of her work. Because of the diversity of her works, Christine de Pizan scholarship has taken many different routes; if at first a great deal of the readings of her were feminist in nature, the scope of Christine studies has broadened to include a wide range of theoretical, historical, and linguistic approaches. While a great deal of the scholarship is in French, she has become increasingly represented in English as well, particularly as women writers were incorporated into medieval literature and survey courses. Willard notes:

> one must know that the time has finally arrived when it is possible to
> view her as an individual of tremendous good will – towards women,

toward France, and toward humanity in general – and as a writer whose complexity is endlessly revealed by a careful reading of all that she wrote.

(Willard 1984: 223)

As the first European author to make a living by her pen – not the first woman author, but the first author – she occupies an important place among medieval (and modern) writers, but it is her poetry that gives her "reason to speak with confidence of her literary immortality" (Willard 1984: 223).

Diversity: 10; Volume: 10; Popularity: 7; Scholarship: 4; Accessibility 4

SIR THOMAS MALORY

England's most comprehensive version of the Arthurian story, *The Morte Darthur*, ends as follows:

I praye you all Jentylmen and jentylwymmen that redeth this book of Arthur and his Knyghhtes from the begynnyng to the endynge, praye for me whyle I am on lyve that God sende me good deluaveraunce. And whan I am deed, I praye you all to praye for my soule.

For this book was ended the ninth yere of the reygne of Kyng Edward the Fourth, by Syr Thomas Maleoré, Kynght, as Jesu help hym for his grete might, as he is the servaunt of jesu both day and nyght.

(Malory 1971: 726)

[I pray you all gentlemen and gentlewomen who read this book of Arthur and his knights from the beginning to the ending, pray for me while I am alive that God send me good deliverance. And when I am dead, I pray you all to pray for my soul.

For this book was ended in the ninth year of the reign of King Edward the Fourth, by Sir Thomas Malory, Knight, as Jesus help him because of his great might, as he is the servant of Jesus both day and night.]

The evidence for the identity of Sir Thomas Malory has remained something of a mystery, although it has been established that he was Knight of Newbold Revel, born between 1400 and 1410 in Warwickshire, who not only fought at Calais in 1436 but became involved late in life on the side of Richard Neville, Earl of Warwick, in the War of the Roses. His infamy as a traitor to King Edward IV does not end there: beginning in 1451, he was jailed eight times, twice escaping by violent means. His body of works, eight romance narratives often known collectively as *Le Morte Darthur* and grouped together as a linked series of narratives, was penned during this time. Debate has continued among scholars, however, as to whether the entire body should be grouped together or viewed as distinct texts. William Caxton's printed version of the text (published first in 1485) differs from the only extant manuscript (known as the Winchester Manuscript, discovered in 1934 and dated c. 1475) and seems to make changes to the chapter rubrics to create a more unified edition of a group of otherwise diverse tales that all center around the Arthurian Court. Because the dates of the Winchester Manuscript and Caxton's printing are so close, Malory is often viewed as the last medieval English writer, and 1485 is thus sometimes considered the end-date of the English Middle Ages, a symbolic suggestion to be sure, and somewhat pointless when considering history, but certainly a useful transitional distinction in thinking about literature given the many literary changes that followed the advent of printing.

Despite the question of whether the *Morte Darthur* is a "hoole booke" or a more diverse collection, Malory is attributed with bringing the legend of Arthur to England in its most complete form. Even if readers have never encountered Malory in his original form, almost everyone is familiar with his stories' contents – most post-medieval versions of the King Arthur story, from Alfred, Lord Tennyson's *Idylls of the King* (1855–85), to novels like T.H. White's *Once and Future King* (1958), to contemporary films like *Excalibur* (1984) and *Monty Python and the Holy Grail* (1978), paintings, plays, operas, and musicals owe a powerful debt to the *Morte Darthur*.

Malory's text owes its own debt to the multiple Arthurian stories that precede him, including Geoffrey of Monmouth's *Historia Regum Britanniae* (c. 1138) and many French romances, especially the *Lancelot-Grail* cycle that, at its heart, is a compilation of the many strands of Arthurian narrative developed since the legend first appeared in Gildas' fifth-century *Chronicles*. However, Malory did not just repeat earlier stories; he made significant alterations to his sources, adding a variety of details and contexts. The diversity of Malory's works (or work) is limited to narratives that focus on the Arthurian Court, yet he offers a wide range of concerns within his stories, often changing the focus of the source stories to align with his narrative interests. Malory added significant military details and an interest in geography that causes him to suggest how long a knight's chivalric quests might take given the conditions of travel. For instance, when Arthur travels through France towards Italy and has a confrontation with the Emperor Lucius of Rome, one distinction that emerges is Malory's clear familiarity with French geography which guides the King's progress. He adds characters to stories and engages with a variety of contemporary issues, particularly military issues. His references to crusading – Arthur fights off a Saracen invasion early in his reign – suggest an anxiety about the potential of invasion by the Ottomans who were expanding their territory during Malory's career, although the most crusade-like event in the poem is the Roman Wars, where Arthur's army fights against an allied army of Europeans and Saracens cast by the text as unclean, uncivilized, and unworthy. Malory sees France as legitimate English territory, a response to the losses of continental power England had suffered since the Battle of Agincourt. Arthur's military right to protect his own land against invaders provides a kind of nationalistic energy in the text, for better or worse, since this often justifies extreme violence and licensed slaughter.

Malory's interest is not solely military; he is also concerned with the necessity and worth of an authentic English hero; the values and precepts of chivalry (and how the notion of courtly love – *fin'amor* – can disrupt it along with those who blindly embrace it); the legend of the Holy Grail; the power of genealogical dynasty; and marriage fidelity. Jill Mann observes that while Malory is a "master at conveying human emotion, and at catching the rhythms of human speech terse or plangent, dignified or touching," he "seems to have little interest in 'character', in the web of emotions and motives that lie behind human speech and action" (Mann 2014: 235). Malory's lack of interest in character may lie behind the *Morte Darthur*'s adaptability into so many post-medieval forms; he leaves absent just what more contemporary writers are eager to fill.

Malory's popularity comes less from his wide current readership (although he is certainly featured in many medieval and Arthurian courses) and more from the vast proliferation of the King Arthur legend that has dominated English history and has worked itself into the fundamental canon of English literature. While Malory himself is not as widely read or known as other medieval authors discussed in this chapter, the unrivaled popularity of the Arthurian legends in all forms earns Malory his place. Adaptations – from the Middle Ages to contemporary times – of the Arthurian tales are too numerous to detail inclusively, but they appear in multiple genres, spanning film, text, drama, poetry, music, art, oral tradition, pseudo-history, graphic novels, and fan fiction. The names of King Arthur, the Holy Grail, Lancelot, and even Guinevere circumnavigate the globe, expanding and evolving, nearly all emerging from Malory's version of these figures – Japanese fans can read King Arthur manga and watch King Arthur anime.

Discrepancies between Caxton's printed version and the Winchester Manuscript pose interesting challenges for Malory scholars, but the work itself is certainly ripe for a variety of contemporary scholarly approaches. While the body of Malory scholarship cannot approach the volume produced about the other authors in this chapter, the *Morte Darthur* has certainly shown itself open to many interpretive interventions. Recent scholarship has examined Malory's martial language, his engagement with chivalry as the institution was waning, gender, wounded bodies, historical memory and consciousness, and the perennial issues of Malory's identity and whether the poem is an anthology or a current whole. Sir John Malory, Knight continues to engage the public as readers of his own text and as consumers of its countless adaptations. Not bad 530 years after his death.

Diversity: 4; Volume: 1; Popularity: 10; Scholarship: 4; Accessibility: 5

SUMMARY

Chaucer cautions his readers in the Miller's Prologue, "men shal nat maken ernest of game" (I. 3186) [A man should not make earnest out of game], and we offer the same suggestion here; in creating our own "Game of Texts" to assess the Middle Ages' most well-known authors, we attempted to create a methodology to explain their popularity beyond their employment of multiple genres (with the exception of Malory). While many medieval authors and texts have achieved a great deal of popularity, these

authors have become iconic in ways others have not. They are sometimes said to have transcended their own times – and yet they are
fundamentally medieval in their concerns, approaches, and methodologies of exploration. Because of their status within the field, and
the difficulty of placing them in any other single chapter since they
generally move comfortably between and among genres, they seemed
to deserve a place of their own. Their own tendencies towards puzzles,
complications, conundrums, games, and knots suggested the game
which governs this chapter; each of these authors appears to take what
might seem particularly medieval forms and complicates them in some
of the ways we have attempted to describe here.

In sum, and to wrap up the competition between each of these
iconic figures, we will give a final tally and determine which
medieval author, according to the criteria we've laid out, can claim
the title of… *the Most Extreme.*

Coming in last place with a total score of 20 is the *Gawain*-poet.

> Fifth place is Thomas Malory with 24.
> Fourth place is Giovanni Boccaccio with 32.
> Third place is Christine de Pizan with 35.
> Second place is Dante Alighieri with 43.
> And, claiming the title of the *Most Extreme Medieval Author* and win-
> ning first place in this Basics Book competition is: Geoffrey Chaucer
> with a total cumulative score of 45 out of 50.

With such a vast variety of works in nearly every genre, and with
an enduring popularity that may have only strengthened with time
among general readers and scholars alike, Chaucer deservedly earns
the title with his wit, his charm, and his insight into the human
condition, explored through comedy, through drama, through epic,
and through sermon. With a well-balanced repertoire, Chaucer
covers all bases and has garnered fame as poet, pioneer, and legend.

FOR FURTHER READING

PRIMARY TEXTS

While all these authors landed in this chapter because of the
diversity of their writing, each one has a work for which he or she

is best known. In Dante's case, *The Divine Comedy* is his master-piece: **Dante Alighieri. (2012).** *The Divine Comedy: Inferno, Purgatory, Paradise.* **Trans. Robin Kirkpatrick. London: Penguin**. Dante's spiritual descendent, Boccaccio, wrote many works but is currently best known for the *Decameron*: **Giovanni Boccaccio. (2003).** *The Decameron.* **Trans. G. H. McWilliam. London: Penguin**, although other works of his had greater influence on the other authors in this chapter.

For Chaucer we have listed the complete works, given how difficult it is to choose between *The Canterbury Tales* and *Troilus and Criseyde*, although the *Tales* are more widely taught: **Geoffrey Chaucer. (2002).** *The Riverside Chaucer,* **3rd Rev. Ed. Ed. Larry D. Benson. Oxford: Oxford University Press**. However, readers who don't want to take on such a big commitment should consider **Geoffrey Chaucer. (2005).** *The Canterbury Tales.* **Ed. Jill Mann. London: Penguin**. We have only provided Chaucer texts in Middle English; the pleasures of learning it are many, and most translations miss out on the richness of Chaucer's language.

Chaucer's near-contemporary is called both the *Pearl*-poet and the *Gawain*-poet, but the latter work is more widely taught and studied: **Sir Gawain and the Green Knight. (2008). Trans. Simon Armitage. New York: W. W. Norton**. There are many good translations, but this recent one by poet and playwright Simon Armitage offers a very poetic style that captures the allit-erative quality of the original. Sir Thomas Malory wrote only one work; appearing in both manuscript and print nearly simulta-neously, it can be seen as a transition between two literary cultures. We have chosen to offer the manuscript version here, since Caxton is known to have changed Malory's text a fair amount: **Sir Thomas Malory. (1998).** *Le Morte Darthur: The Winchester Manuscript.* **Ed. Helen Cooper. Oxford: Oxford University Press**.

Like Boccaccio, Christine de Pizan wrote a wide range of works in different genres (and was indeed influenced by Boccaccio in several of them); however, her best known and most taught work remains *The Book of the City of Ladies*, which is a good place to begin an exploration of her prolific career: **Christine de Pizan. (1982).** *The Book of the City of Ladies.* **Ed. and Trans. Earl Jeffrey Richards. New York: Persea**.

SECONDARY SOURCES

Because of the importance of these authors and the range of their works, it is difficult to choose what works of criticism to offer here. For some authors, such as Chaucer, there are many good basic volumes, while for others superb criticism exists, but it is much more textually specific. Here we have chosen one work on each author that we find useful. For Dante we have chosen **Teodolinda Barolini. (1992).** *The Undivine Comedy: Detheologizing Dante.* **Princeton, NJ: Princeton University Press**, because it invites readers to examine the text politically as well as theologically and consider the secular elements of Dante's seemingly religious work. For Chaucer, among the very fine guides to his work is: **Tison Pugh. (2013).** *An Introduction to Geoffrey Chaucer.* **Gainesville, FL: University Press of Florida**, which offers a comprehensive overview of Chaucer, almost an entire Chaucer course in a single volume. Another valuable introduction is *The Cambridge Introduction to Chaucer* (2014). **Ed. Alistair Minnis. Cambridge: Cambridge University Press**, which also brings readers into the breadth and depth of Chaucer's work. *The Cambridge Companion to Boccaccio* (2015). **Ed. Guyda Armstrong, Rhiannon Daniels, and Stephen J. Milner. Cambridge: Cambridge University Press**, explores Boccaccio as scholar, interpreter of the classics, and innovative author deserving of equal status to Petrarch and Dante. Although somewhat specific in its focus, *Malory and Christianity: Essays on Sir Thomas Malory's* **Morte Darthur** (2013), **Ed. D. Thomas Hanks, Jr. and Janet Jesmok. Kalamazoo, MI: Medieval Institute Publications** collects a series of essays by contemporary scholars that focus on Malory's tragic and romance elements, focusing on the human qualities of the work. **Derek Brewer and John Gibson's** *A Companion to the Gawain-Poet* (1997). **Cambridge: D. S. Brewer** similarly offers a range of essays on the poet and his works, and it has the advantage of also being available online through Google Books: https://books.google.com/books?id=t3VssvC5VEwC&printsec=front cover&source=gbs_ge_summary_r&cad=0#v=onepage&q&f=false. Also available online is **R. A. Shoaf's** *The Poem as Green Girdle:* **Commercium** *in* **Sir Gawain and the Green Knight.** **(1984). Gainesville, FL: University Press of Florida:**http://

users.clas.ufl.edu/ras/gawain/masterng.htm, which views the poem through its methodologies of exchange – very appropriate for this chapter on games. Finally, an introduction to Christine de Pizan can be found in **Nadia Margolis. (2012).** *An Introduction to Christine de Pizan.* **Gainesville, FL: University Press of Florida**, which provides a route into Christine de Pizan's entire corpus and examines themes and issues that appear across the range of her texts.

WEB RESOURCES

Medievalists might not seem like a group that would take to the Internet naturally, but in fact, medieval resources have been available since early in its history, and they have continued to develop as technology becomes more sophisticated and makes the sharing of images, ideas, and texts increasingly possible. We have listed here a variety of resources that provide perspectives, backgrounds, and access to medieval materials. The list is not exhaustive by any means, but like the rest of this volume, offers a place to start one's inquiry.

Two particularly interesting blogs written by medievalists about the uses (and abuses) of the Middle Ages in the contemporary world are:

In the Medieval Middle: www.inthemedievalmiddle.com/ a medieval studies group blog written by several major scholars in the field, including guest bloggers; while they address the Middle Ages in the contemporary world, they provide a very thoughtful sense of the field.

The Public Medievalist: www.publicmedievalist.com/ a web-magazine focusing on the intersections of medieval history, modern politics, and culture. Its articles and special series cover a wide range of topics and are written by major scholars in the field.

FOR TEXTS AND RESOURCES:

The *Internet Medieval Sourcebook:* https://sourcebooks.fordham.edu/sbook.asp has unfortunately stopped being updated, but it still offers an enormous range of texts and resources from all aspects of medieval life.

Monastic Matrix: https://monasticmatrix.osu.edu/ offers primary texts and secondary sources, biographies, images, and vocabulary for the study of medieval religious women.

Feminae: http://inpress.lib.uiowa.edu/feminae/. Produced by the Society for Medieval Feminist Scholarship, Feminae indexes journal articles, book reviews, and essays in books about women, sexuality, and gender during the Middle Ages.

Luminarium: www.luminarium.org/medlit/ offers an Anthology of Medieval English literature from 1350–1485, providing links to texts, resources, and background materials.

Netserf: The Internet Connection for Medieval Resources: www.net serf.org/ is a search engine attempting to provide a single index for all aspects of medieval studies on the Web.

In Parentheses: www.yorku.ca/inpar/ is a library of medieval texts from a wide range of traditions; the site offers many texts from outside of Europe and the Middle East, as well as more commonly available works.

The Online Medieval and Classical Library: http://omacl.org/ makes available editions and translations of many medieval and Classical texts, sorted by genre, author, and language.

The Camelot Project: http://d.lib.rochester.edu/camelot-project is an excellent resource for all things King Arthur, medieval and modern.

FOR SOME USEFUL RESOURCES ON SPECIFIC AUTHORS:

Danteworlds: http://danteworlds.laits.utexas.edu offers a multimedia exploration of the *Divine Comedy*, including text, images, and audio recordings that allow a visual experience of the poem, while also providing valuable notes on the various figures and characters that Dante encounters as he travels through the afterlife.

Digital Dante: https://digitaldante.columbia.edu/, a product of Columbia University in New York, offers English translations and Italian editions of Dante's works, focusing on the *Divine Comedy*. One of its useful offerings is a searchable intertextual edition of the poem.

Harvard Chaucer Page: http://sites.fas.harvard.edu/~chaucer/ from Harvard University provides biographical material, a chronology of Chaucer's work, texts in translation and the original Middle English, helpful information for reading Chaucer's English, historical background, and a searchable glossary.

Online Chaucer Bibliography: www.library.ucsb.edu/research/db/1129 is a comprehensive, searchable database of research on Chaucer.

Chaucer Doth Tweet: https://twitter.com/LeVostreGC and Geoffrey Chaucer Hath a Blog: https://houseoffame.blogspot.com/ give students a lively opportunity to practice Middle English as they read "Chaucer's" thoughts on the contemporary world, his rivalry with John Gower, popular music, film, and television, and all manner of advice.

Decameron Web: www.brown.edu/Departments/Italian_Studies/dweb/ provides resources for studying Boccaccio, including background, texts, translations, and maps.

FOR MEDIEVALISM:

Medieval Afterlives: https://medievalafterlives.wordpress.com/. This blog is companion to the book *Medieval Afterlives in Contemporary Cultures* and provides information for consumers of medievalisms.

Medievally Speaking: http://medievallyspeaking.blogspot.com/ engages critically with all scholarly investigations of and creative commentary on the continuing process of creating the Middle Ages, mostly with reviews and review essays, but also with interviews from an international body of scholars.

BIBLIOGRAPHY

Abrams, M. H. and Geoffrey Galt Harpham. (2014) "Fabliau." *A Glossary of Literary Terms*. 11th Edition. New York: Cengage, p. 122.

Armstrong, Elizabeth Psakis. (1994) "Julian of Norwich (1342–circa 1420)." *Old and Middle English Literature*. Ed. Jeffrey Helterman and Jerome Mitchell. Vol. 146. Detroit: Gale, pp. 211–216.

Ashton, Gail, ed. (2015) *Medieval Afterlives in Contemporary Cultures*. London: Bloomsbury Academic.

Auerbach, Erich. (1953) "The Knight Sets Forth." *Mimesis*. Trans. Willard Trask. Princeton, NJ: Princeton University Press, pp. 132–142.

Augustine. (1991) *Confessions*. Trans. Henry Chadwick. New York: Oxford University Press.

Augustine. (2010) *On the Free Choice of the Will, On Grace and Free Choice, and Other Writings*. Ed. and Trans. Peter King. New York: Cambridge University Press.

Batts, Michael S. (1992) "Gottfried von Strassburg (died before 1230)." *German Writers and Works of the High Middle Ages, 1170–1280*. Ed. James N. Hardin and Will Hasty. Vol. 138. Detroit: Gale, pp. 16–26.

Baugh, Albert C. (1967) *A Literary History of England*. London: Routledge.

Benedict of Nursia. (1960) *The Rule of St. Benedict*. Trans. E. F. Henderson. *Introduction to Contemporary Civilization in the West*. Ed. The Contemporary Civilization Staff of Columbia College. Vol. I, 3rd Edition. New York: Columbia University Press.

Bergin, Thomas G. (1965) *Dante*. Boston: Houghton Mifflin.

Bloch, R. Howard. (1983) *Etymologies and Genealogies: A Literary Anthropology of the French Middle Ages*. Chicago: University of Chicago Press.

Boccaccio, Giovanni. (1994) *Il Corbaccio*. Ed. Giorgio Padoan. From *Tutte le opere di Giovanni Boccaccio*, 12 vols, ed. by Vittore Branca. Milan: Mondadori, 1964–, V (ii), pp. 413–614.

Bosco, Umberto. (2014) "Giovanni Boccaccio: Italian Poet and Scholar." *Encyclopaedia Brittanica.* 19 November 2014. www.britannica.com/biograp hy/Giovanni-Boccaccio Accessed: 8 May 2017.

Brown, Katherine Adams. (2014) *Boccaccio's Fabliaux: Medieval Short Stories and the Function of Reversal.* Gainesville: University Press of Florida.

Brown, Katherine DeVane. (2015) "Courtly Rivalry, Loyalty Conflict, and the Figure of Hagen in the Nibelungenlied." *Montashefte* 107:3, 355–381.

Brown University Italian Studies Department. (2014) "Some Critical Questions About the Corbaccio." *Decameron Web, Brown University.* 30 January 2014. www.brown.edu/Departments/Italian_Studies/dweb/texts/corbaccio/crit. shtml Accessed: 8 May 2017.

Bruckner, Matilda Tomaryn. (1999) "Marie de France (flourished 1160–1178)." *Literature of the French and Occitan Middle Ages: Eleventh to Fifteenth Centuries.* Ed. Deborah M. Sinnreich-Levi and Ian S. Laurie. Vol. 208. Detroit: Gale, pp. 199–208.

Capellanus, Andreas. (1941) *The Art of Courtly Love.* Trans. John Jay Parry. New York: W. W. Norton and Co.

Chabaneau, Camile. (1855) *Les biographies des troubadours en langue provençale.* Toulouse: Eduouard Privat.

Chaucer, Geoffrey. (1987) *The Riverside Chaucer.* Ed. Larry D. Benson. Boston: Houghton Mifflin.

Christine de Pisan. (1982) *The Book of the City of Ladies.* Trans. Earl Jeffrey Richards. New York: Persea Books.

Christine de Pisan. (1999) *The Book of Deeds of Arms and of Chivalry.* Trans. Sumner Willard, Ed. Charity Cannon Willard. University Park, PA: University of Pennsylvania Press.

Ciabattari, Jane. (2014) "Why is Rumi the Best-Selling Poet in the US?" *BBC Culture.* 21 October 2014. www.bbc.com/culture/story/20140414-americas-best-selling-poet. Accessed: 1 September 2017.

Contemporary Civilization Staff of Columbia College (Ed.) (1960) *Introduction to Contemporary Civilization in the West.* Vol. I, 3rd Edition. New York: Columbia University Press.

Crawford, Dan D. (1988) "Intellect and Will in Augustine's Confessions." *Religious Studies* 24:3, pp. 291–302.

Deam, Lisa. (2015) *A World Transformed: Exploring the Spirituality of Medieval Maps.* Eugene, OR: Cascade Publishing.

Despres, Denise L. (1994) "Margery Kempe (circa 1373–1438)." *Old and Middle English Literature.* Ed. Jeffrey Helterman and Jerome Mitchell. Vol. 146. Detroit: Gale, pp. 217–221.

Donaldson, E. Talbot. (1970) *Speaking of Chaucer.* New York: W. W. Norton and Co.

Duby, Georges. (1983) *The Knight, the Lady, and the Priest: The Making of Modern Marriage in Medieval France*. Trans. Barbara Bray. New York: Pantheon.

Duby, Georges. (1992) "The Courtly Model." Trans. Arthur Goldhammer. *A History of Women in the West: Silences of the Middle Ages*. Ed. Christine Klapisch-Zuber. Cambridge, MA: Belknap Press of Harvard University Press, pp. 250–266.

Fleteren, Frederick Van. (1992) "Augustine (13 November 354–28 August 430)." *Medieval Philosophers*. Ed. Jeremiah Hackett. Vol. 115. Detroit: Gale, pp. 53–67.

Gardner, Miranda. (2016) "Imagining Ovid and Chrétien in Fourteenth-Century French Libraries." *French Studies* 70:2, pp. 201–215.

Geoffrey of Monmouth. (1966) *History of the Kings of Britain*. Trans. Lewis Thorpe. London: Penguin.

Geoffroi de Charny. (1996) *The Book of Chivalry*. Trans. Richard W. Kaeuper and Elspeth Kennedy. Philadelphia: University of Pennsylvania Press.

Giovanni Boccaccio. (1964–) 12 vols, ed. by Vittore Branca. Milan: Mondadori, V (ii). www.brown.edu/Departments/Italian_Studies/dweb/texts/corba ccio/crit.shtml Accessed: 8 May 2017.

Goldsmith, Margaret E. (1962) "The Christian Perspective in *Beowulf*." *Comparative Literature* 14:1, pp. 71–90.

Griffin, Miranda. (2015) *Transforming Tales: Rewriting Metamorphosis in Old French Literature*. Oxford: Oxford University Press.

Guillame d'Orange. (1974) Ed. Joan M. Ferrante. New York: Columbia University Press.

Hala, James. (1999) "Bernard of Clairvaux (1090–20 August 1153)." *Literature of French and Occitan Middle Ages: Eleventh to Fifteenth Centuries*. Ed. Deborah M. Sinnreich-Levi and Ian S. Laurie. Vol. 208. Detroit: Gale, pp. 27–36.

Hanning, Robert W. (1977) *The Individual in Twelfth-Century Romance*. New Haven: Yale University Press.

Harlequin Romance Writers Guidelines – Desire Series. Harlequin Romance. https://harlequin.submittable.com/submit. Accessed: 1 August 2016.

Hasty, Will. (1994) "Hartmann von Aue (circa 1160–circa 1205)." *German Writers and Works of the High Middle Ages, 1170–1280*. Ed. James N. Hardin and Will Hasty. Vol. 138. Detroit: Gale, pp. 27–43.

Hawkins, Peter S. (2006) *Dante: A Brief History*. Malden, MA: Blackwell.

Helterman, Jeffrey. (1994) "Geoffrey Chaucer (1340?–1400)." *Old and Middle English Literature*. Ed. Jeffrey Helterman and Jerome Mitchell. Vol. 146. Detroit: Gale, pp. 127–144.

Heng, Geraldine. (2003) *Empire of Magic: Medieval Romance and the Politics of Cultural Fantasy*. New York: Columbia University Press.

Howard, Donald. (1980) *Writers and Pilgrims: Medieval Pilgrimage Narratives and their Posterity*. Berkeley, CA: University of California Press.

Hunt, Patrick. (2011) "Biography of Dante." *Critical Insights: The Inferno.* Pasadena, CA: Salem Press, pp. 20–27.

Ibn-Battutah. (2002) *The Travels of Ibn Battutah.* Ed. and Trans. Tim Mackintosh-Smith. London: Picador.

Kaeuper, Richard. (1999) *Chivalry and Violence in Medieval Europe.* Oxford: Oxford University Press.

Karkov, Catherine E. (2003) "Tales of the Ancients: Colonial Werewolves and the Mapping of Post-Colonial Ireland." *Postcolonial Moves: Medieval through Modern.* Ed. Patricia Clare Ingham and Michelle R. Warren. New York and London: Palgrave Macmillan, pp. 95–99.

Krueger, Roberta L. (2000) "Introduction." *The Cambridge Companion to Medieval Romance.* Ed. Roberta L. Krueger. Cambridge: Cambridge University Press, pp. 1–9.

Llull, Ramon. (2013) *The Book of the Order of Chivalry.* Trans. Noel Fallows. Woodbridge: Boydell Press.

Luria, Maxwell S. and Richard L. Hoffman, eds. and trans. (1974) *Middle English Lyrics.* New York: W. W. Norton and Co.

Maalouf, Amin. (1984) *The Crusades Through Arab Eyes.* Trans. John Rothschild. New York: Schocken Books.

Mandeville, Sir John. (2005) *The Tales of Sir John Mandeville.* Ed. and Trans. C. W. R. D. Moseley. London: Penguin.

Malory, Sir Thomas. (1971) *Works.* Ed. Eugène Vinaver. Oxford: Oxford University Press.

Mann, Jill. (2014) "Knightly Combat in Malory's Morte d'Arthur." *Life in Words: Essays on Chaucer, the Gawain-Poet, and Malory.* Toronto: University of Toronto Press.

Marco Polo. (2014–2015). Written and Created by John Fusco. Netflix/the Weinstein Company.

Marie de France. (1978) *The Lais of Marie de France.* Trans. Robert Hanning and Joan Ferrante. Durham, NC: Labyrinth Press.

Matarasso, Pauline M. (2005) "Introduction." *The Quest of the Holy Grail.* London: Penguin.

Mazzotta, Giuseppe. (1986) *The World at Play in Boccaccio's Decameron.* Princeton, NJ: Princeton University Press, pp. 9–30.

McKeon, Michael. (1987) *The Rise of the English Novel 1600–1740.* Baltimore: Johns Hopkins University Press.

Muscatine, Charles. (1986). *The Old French Fabliaux.* New Haven, CT: Yale University Press.

Nolan, Barbara. (1992) *Chaucer and the Tradition of the Romans Antiques.* Cambridge: Cambridge University Press.

Papio, Michael, ed. and trans. (2009) *Boccaccio's Expositions on Dante's Comedy.* Toronto: University of Toronto Press.

Parker, Patricia. (1979) *Inescapable Romance: Studies in the Poetics of a Mode.* Princeton, NJ: Princeton University Press.

Petroff, Elizabeth Avilda, ed. (1986) *Medieval Women's Visionary Literature.* Oxford: Oxford University Press.

Petroff, Elizabeth Avilda, ed. (1991) "The Mystics." *Christianity Today* 30. www.christianitytoday.com/history/issues/issue-30/mystics.html. Accessed: 5 May 2017.

Polo, Marco. (2016) *The Description of the World.* Ed. and Trans. Sharon Kinoshita. Indianapolis: Hackett.

Reynolds, Barbara. (2006) *Dante: The Poet, the Political Thinker, the Man.* Emeryville, CA: Shoemaker & Hoard, an imprint of Avalon Pub. Group.

Ross, Alex. (2003) "The Ring and the Rings: Wagner vs. Tolkien." *The New Yorker.* www.newyorker.com/magazine/2003/12/22/the-ring-and-the-rings. Accessed: 26 February 2017.

Saunders, Corrine J. (1993) *The Forest of Medieval Romance: Avernus, Broceliande, Arden.* Cambridge: D. S. Brewer.

Seaman, Gerald. (1999) "Chrétien de Troyes (circa 1140–circa 1190)." *Literature of the French and Occitan Middle Ages: Eleventh to Fifteenth Centuries.* Ed. Deborah M. Sinnreich-Levi and Ian S. Laurie. Vol. 208. Detroit: Gale, pp. 72–85.

Shippey, Tom. (n.d.) "Medievalism." *Studies in Medievalism* website. www.medievalism.net/conferences/ Accessed: 28 August 2017.

The Siege of Jerusalem. (2003) Ed. Ralph Hanna and David Lawton. Oxford: Early English Text Society.

Shoaf, R. A. (1984) *The Poem as Green Girdle: Commercium in Sir Gawain and the Green Knight.* Gainesville: University of Florida Press.

Sir Gawain and the Green Knight, Pearl, and Sir Orfeo. (1975) Trans. J. R. R. Tolkien. London: Allen and Unwin.

Sir Gawain and the Green Knight: A New Verse Translation. (2002) Trans. W. S. Merwin. New York: Alfred A. Knopf.

Sir Gawain and the Green Knight: A New Verse Translation. (2008) Trans. Simon Armitage. New York: W. W. Norton.

"The 21-Second Excitation." (2010) *The Big Bang Theory*, season 4, episode 8. Mark Cendrowski, dir. Warner Bros. Television.

"The Decameron." (2013) *Publisher's Weekly.* www.publishersweekly.com/978-0-393-06930-3. 22 July 2013. Accessed: 10 June 2017.

The Travels of Sir John Mandeville. (2005) Ed. and Trans. C. W. R. D. Moseley. London: Penguin.

Tolkien, J. R. R. (1983) "On Fairy-Stories." *The Monsters and the Critics and Other Essays,* Ed. Christopher Tolkien. London: George Allen and Unwin, pp. 109–161.

Turchi, Peter. (2004) *Maps of the Imagination: The Writer as Cartographer.* San Antonio, TX: Trinity University Press.

Van Duzer, Chet. (2013) *Sea Monsters on Medieval and Renaissance Maps*. London: British Library.

Vinaver, Eugene. (1971) *The Rise of Romance*. Oxford: Clarendon Press.

Watt, Ian. (1957) *The Rise of the Novel*. London: Chatto and Windus.

Weisl, Angela Jane. (1995) *Conquering the Reign of Femeny: Gender and Genre in Chaucer's Romance*. Cambridge: D. S. Brewer.

Wheeler, Kip. (2017) "Epic." *Literary Terms and Definitions: E*. http://web.cn.edu/kwheeler/lit_terms_E.html. Accessed: 28 August 2017.

Willard, Charity Cannon. (1984) *Christine de Pizan: Her Life and Works*. New York: Persea Books.

Willibald. *Life of St. Boniface by Wilibald*. (1916) Trans. George Washington Robinson. Cambridge, MA: Harvard University Press. Available on the *Internet Medieval Sourcebook*: https://sourcebooks.fordham.edu/basis/willibald-boniface.asp. Accessed: 8 May 2017.

Wilson, Katherina, ed. and trans. (1985) *The Dramas of Hrostvit of Gandersheim*. Toronto: Peregrina.

Wilson, Katherina, ed. (1998) *Hrotsvit of Gandersheim: A Florilegium of her Works*. Cambridge: D. S. Brewer.

Wynn, Marianne. (1994) "Wolfram von Eschenbach (circa 1179–after 1220)." *German Writers and Works of the High Middle Ages*. Ed. James N. Hardin and Will Hasty. Vol. 138. Detroit: Gale, pp. 185–206.

INDEX